READING COMPREHENSION
FOR GIRLS
Julie Harper

Reading Comprehension for Girls
48 Fun Short Stories

Copyright © 2014 Julie Harper
wackysentences.com

Cover design and illustrations by Melissa Stevens
www.theillustratedauthor.net
Write. Create. Illustrate.

All rights are reserved by the author, including the right to reproduce any portion of this workbook in any form, with the following exceptions:

☺ Any teacher who purchases one copy of the print edition of this book may reproduce selected activities for all of his or her own classes.

☺ Any parent who purchases one copy of the print edition of this book may reproduce selected activities for all of his or her own immediate family members.

These stories are fictional works. Names and characters are products of the author's imagination; any resemblance to actual persons, living or dead, is entirely by coincidence.

Children's Books > Education & Reference > Reading & Writing
Children's Books > Literature & Fiction > Short Story Collections

ISBN-10: 1500860654
ISBN-13: 978-1500860653

BRIEF CONTENTS

Introduction	v
Part 1: Stories 1–16 (1 page each)	7
Part 2: Stories 17–32 (1–2 pages each)	41
Part 3: Stories 33–48 (2–3 pages each)	91
Answer Key	155

STORY LIST

Introduction
Part 1: Stories 1– 16 (1 page each)
    Story #1: Treasure Hunt
    Story #2: Riding a Cloud
    Story #3: Three Wishes
    Story #4: Dream Fairies
    Story #5: Basketball Girl
    Story #6: Lucky Penny
    Story #7: Mermaid Swim
    Story #8: Fairyland
    Story #9: Rescue Cat
    Story #10: Star Gazer
    Story #11: Princess of the Year
    Story #12: Field Trip
    Story #13: Fairy Night
    Story #14: Dolphin Swim
    Story #15: Pool Party
    Story #16: Dream Flight
Part 2: Stories 17– 32 (1– 2 pages each)
    Story #17: Rainbow Fairy
    Story #18: Slumber Party
    Story #19: Golden Eagle
    Story #20: Sweet Land
    Story #21: Mermaid Friend
    Story #22: Robot Design
    Story #23: Birthday Surprise
    Story #24: Harsh Words
    Story #25: Best Friend
    Story #26: Water Park
    Story #27: Royal Feast
    Story #28: Magic Bike
    Story #29: Camping Scare
    Story #30: Fashion Design
    Story #31: Magic Time
    Story #32: Special Glasses

Part 3: Stories 33– 48 (2– 3 pages each)
    Story #33: Mrs. Crabtree
    Story #34: Island Magic
    Story #35: Royal Ball— Part 1
    Story #36: Royal Ball— Part 2
    Story #37: Royal Ball— Part 3
    Story #38: Slumber Mystery
    Story #39: County Fair
    Story #40: Mermaid Surprise— Part 1
    Story #41: Mermaid Surprise— Part 2
    Story #42: Mermaid Surprise— Part 3
    Story #43: Martian Guide
    Story #44: Fairy World
    Story #45: Magic Carpet
    Story #46: The King's Ball
    Story #47: Glass-bottom Boat
    Story #48: Reading Club
Answer Key

INTRODUCTION

The goal of this reading comprehension book is to encourage girls to read—and practice understanding what they have read—through 48 fun short stories about topics that many girls can relate to, including stories about fairies, mermaids, princesses, slumber parties, magic items, birthday parties, field trips, and more.

This book begins with 1-page stories (~200-300 words), progresses to stories with 1-2 pages (~300-400 words), and concludes with stories with 2-3 pages (~500-800 words).

Each story is followed by four multiple choice questions designed to test how well students comprehend the story. Students who have read the story and who understand what they have read should be able to answer the questions correctly. The multiple choice questions in Part 1 have about three answers to choose from, while those in Part 3 have about five answers to choose from.

Correct answers to every question can be found in the answer key at the back of the book. The answer key helps parents or teachers quickly check the answers, and can also be used as a self-check by students who are working independently.

Although these short stories were put together in the form of a reading comprehension book, the reading questions are, of course, optional. These could also serve as bedtime stories or leisure reading, for example.

If a student is struggling to answer the questions correctly, it may be helpful for a parent or teacher to listen to the student read one or more stories and discuss the story with the student. Personal interactions in this way can help the student build confidence in reading and learn how to reason out the answers.

The print edition of this book includes lined space in which students should summarize the stories of Parts 1-2. Assigning these summaries will force students to read the full story instead of just searching through the text to quickly find the answers to the questions. It would also be good writing composition practice.

May your children or students learn to love reading and may they make reading a lifelong habit! ☺

PART 1

Stories 1-16 (1 page each)

Story #1

Treasure Hunt

We went on a scavenger hunt at Alexia's birthday party. We were told that there were several clues leading to a hidden treasure. It was a team adventure. We had to work together.

The first clue was, "It is freezing cold in here." We quickly ran to the kitchen and opened the freezer.

There we found the second clue: "Alexia rests her head here at night." Off we ran to her bedroom.

We discovered the third clue under a pillow on Alexia's bed. It read: "It has eighty-eight keys." With a little thought, we dashed off to the living room where the piano was.

The next clue said, "In the winter, it can get really hot in here." "Um," we said in unison. Since it was summertime, it took a little thought to remember that we use a fireplace in the winter.

We found another clue on the fireplace mantle. "Alexia's favorite drink is found here." This time we quickly ran to the kitchen and opened the refrigerator.

The last clue was taped to a carton of lemonade. It was a map that led to a treasure chest. The map led us from the refrigerator to the front door. It then led to Alexia's backyard. Once in the backyard, it showed us to follow the brick pathway. On the map, an X was marked at the end of the pathway. We ran to the end of the pathway. Wow! We found a large decorated treasure chest.

The map told us to take the treasure chest to Alexia's living room where we could open it and share the treasure. The chest was filled with toys and candies.

Summarize the story in the space provided.

_____

_____

_____

_____

1. The _____ had eighty-eight keys.
    (A) computer keyboard
    (B) organ
    (C) piano

2. The map was found _____.
    (A) at the end of the pathway
    (B) on the carton of lemonade
    (C) on the fireplace mantle

3. The chest was found _____.
    (A) at the end of the pathway
    (B) in Alexia's living room
    (C) in the refrigerator

4. Who got the treasure?
    (A) Alexia
    (B) Alexia's best friend
    (C) everyone shared it

Part 1: Stories 1–16 (1 page each)

Story #2

Riding a Cloud

I climbed a hill so that I could be in a cloud. I kept climbing until I reached the top of the cloud. I looked down and saw my friends waving to me. The cloud started rising upward. I found myself riding the cloud. The cloud kept rising higher and higher until I felt like I was touching the sky.

The cloud was soft to my touch. I wondered what it tasted like. Yummy! It was cotton candy.

It was exciting to look at everything down below. The cloud took me over an amusement park. I could see kids riding a Ferris wheel, roller coaster, merry-go-round, and other rides. The roller coaster didn't look so big and scary from up high.

There was so much water. There were many ponds, rivers, lakes, and even swimming pools. When the cloud took me over the ocean, I wondered when I would see land again. When I passed a huge cruise ship, I waved to the passengers on board.

My favorite site was a castle in England. I blew a kiss to a princess, and she waved and smiled at me.

I knew it was time for me to go home. When the cloud reached a rainbow, I stepped off the cloud onto the rainbow. Whee! I slid down the rainbow and landed in my backyard.

Summarize the story in the space provided.

_____

_____

_____

_____

1. What did the cloud taste like?
    (A) a snow cone
    (B) cotton candy
    (C) vanilla ice-cream

2. The girl on the cloud blew a kiss to _____.
    (A) a princess
    (B) her friends
    (C) her mother

3. The girl climbed the hill to _____.
    (A) be in a cloud
    (B) get away
    (C) see a castle

4. Which site was the girl's favorite?
    (A) a castle
    (B) her backyard
    (C) the rainbow

Part 1: Stories 1–16 (1 page each)

Story #3

Three Wishes

Angie and her mother went shopping for antiques one morning. Angie spotted a beautiful silver bottle. Angie was very excited when her mother bought the bottle for her.

Later that day, Angie was softly rubbing the bottle as she showed it to her friend, Jody. Strange noises came out of the bottle. Suddenly, a genie popped out of the bottle. The genie said, "Hello. You are my master now. I will grant you three wishes."

Angie and Jody started giggling so hard that Angie almost dropped the bottle. They looked at each other, not believing what they heard. Jody told Angie to go ahead and make a wish.

Angie said, "Genie, please clean my room for me."

Poof! Her room was magically cleaned.

"Wow! That was incredible! For my next wish, please do my homework for me."

Poof! Her homework was done.

"This is fun! Genie, for my third wish, I would like to have my own candy shop."

Poof! Her room turned into a candy shop.

Angie asked if she could have one more wish, but the genie was back in the bottle and didn't answer her. Why didn't she just ask for the most important thing in life, happiness? Now all she had was a room full of more candy than she could ever eat.

Summarize the story in the space provided.

_____

_____

_____

_____

1. Who bought the bottle?
    (A) Angie
    (B) Angie's mother
    (C) Jody

2. What color was the bottle?
    (A) gold
    (B) silver
    (C) white

3. What was Angie's second wish?
    (A) a candy shop
    (B) to clean her room
    (C) to finish her homework

4. Angie regrets not wishing for _____.
    (A) candy
    (B) happiness
    (C) money

Part 1: Stories 1-16 (1 page each)

Story #4

Dream Fairies

My cat's name is Charlie. I like to call her CC. It's short for Charlie Cat.

One day CC looked me in the eyes and the strangest thing happened. It was like I could read her mind. She said that she wanted to show me something. She told me that while she was out roaming, she found a secret place. She was sure I would want to see it. Of course I did!

I followed CC throughout our neighborhood to a hidden garden of waterfalls and colorful flowers. Pretty fairies came up to us. One of the fairies gave me a tiara made of pink flowers. The same fairy gave CC a little tiara made from yellow flowers.

We sat in the garden and sang songs. We ate yummy sweet cakes and drank fruit punch.

I couldn't believe that CC had found this lovely secret spot, and was sharing it with me. It was close to my home, but I had never seen it before.

Suddenly, I heard an alarm ringing. I looked around, and saw that I was in my own bed. Where was my tiara? Had it all just been a dream? I called CC. She meowed and licked my face. I asked her about the secret garden. She just looked at me and meowed again.

Summarize the story in the space provided.

_____

_____

_____

_____

1. What color was the girl's tiara?
    (A) pink
    (B) red
    (C) yellow

2. What is the cat's name?
    (A) CC for Charlie Cat
    (B) CC for Curious Cat
    (C) CC for Cutie Cat

3. The cat took the girl to _____.
    (A) a cake shop
    (B) a hidden garden
    (C) their backyard

4. Was it all just a dream?
    (A) yes
    (B) no

Story #5

Basketball Girl

Sophia loved playing basketball, but she spent most of the time sitting on the bench. The other girls didn't want her on their team because she was shorter than they were. Sophia was determined to prove that basketball isn't just about height. She just needed one chance to show them how good she was.

Every night, Sophia practiced dribbling the ball. She quickly advanced the ball up and down the court.

Sophia's big chance came one game when two of the regular players were out sick. Sophia knew she had to play her best. She was quick on her feet. Every time she got the ball, she quickly dribbled it down the court. She either made a basket or passed it to one of her teammates.

Sophia's teammates were impressed with how well she was playing. They were rooting her on. Sophia heard them yelling, "Go, Sophia!" Sophia was very excited. She was finally able to play in a real game. She was showing the girls on her team that she could play well, too.

Sophia's team won! Yeah! Her teammates all gathered around her. They told her what a good player she was. They couldn't believe how she quickly dribbled the ball down the court and how many baskets they made with her help. They even wanted her to be one of the regular starters from then on.

Sophia's basketball dream had come true.

Summarize the story in the space provided.

_____
_____
_____
_____

1. What was Sophia's favorite sport?
    (A) baseball
    (B) basketball
    (C) softball

2. How did Sophia get her chance to play?
    (A) It was her turn.
    (B) She asked politely.
    (C) Two girls were out sick.

3. Sophia's advantage was that she was _____.
    (A) quick
    (B) tall
    (C) the captain

4. Did being short prevent Sophia from playing basketball well?
    (A) yes
    (B) no

Story #6

Lucky Penny

I once found a lucky penny. How do I know that it's lucky? Ever since I picked it up, I have been having really good luck.

The first stroke of luck happened when my dad gave me two dollars. Since the next day was my little sister's birthday, I used the money to buy her a chocolate cupcake.

Another lucky thing happened when I heard that a carnival was coming to our town. My mom told me that we could buy tickets if I finished my homework. I knew the carnival would be really fun. I finished my homework quickly, and my mom bought the tickets.

The third lucky thing happened to me when I called my friend, Kelly. I told Kelly that we were buying tickets to the carnival. She told me that she would be going to the carnival too because she had finished her homework.

We had a great day at the carnival. The rides were exciting. The games were fun. The snacks were delicious.

When I showed my teacher, Miss Daisy, my lucky penny, she asked me what was lucky about it. I told her the three lucky things that happened to me after I found it.

Miss Daisy asked me how often my dad gives me money. I told her that I get two dollars when I finish my chores.

"So," Miss Daisy said, "the two dollars was for your allowance. That wasn't a stroke of luck. You and Kelly both worked hard to get your homework done. That was hard work, not luck."

Summarize the story in the space provided.

_____

_____

_____

_____

1. The girl spent two dollars on _____.
   - (A) a cupcake
   - (B) a swing
   - (C) carnival tickets

2. Why did the girl get two dollars?
   - (A) birthday money
   - (B) her allowance
   - (C) her penny was lucky

3. Why did the girls go to the carnival?
   - (A) The penny was lucky.
   - (B) Their allowance paid for it.
   - (C) They finished their homework.

4. Was it really a lucky penny?
   - (A) yes
   - (B) no

Part 1: Stories 1–16 (1 page each)

Story #7

Mermaid Swim

Susie loves swimming in the ocean. She has always dreamed of swimming with a mermaid.

One summer day, her wish came true. She was swimming along the shore when she met a cute mermaid named Meredith. Meredith loves exploring the ocean and has many ocean friends. Meredith invited Susie to swim with her. They first explored the coral reefs. The coral reefs and sea life were breathtaking.

Meredith introduced Susie to a porpoise named Paul. Paul loves riding the waves. Paul asked the girls to swim along with him. Then Paul let Susie ride on his back. That was very exciting.

Meredith and Paul took Susie to meet a sea turtle named Timmy. Paul and Timmy took turns letting Susie ride on their backs. Susie was impressed with their swimming skills.

Meredith suggested that they take Susie to their favorite cave. Susie had never seen a cave before. It was really dark, but Meredith had a flashlight. She led the way and introduced Susie to creatures that live in the dark cave. Susie met cavefish. She was surprised to learn that cavefish are blind.

What an extraordinary day! Susie got to swim with a mermaid, porpoise, and a sea turtle.

Summarize the story in the space provided.

_____

_____

_____

_____

1. Who is Meredith?
   (A) a mermaid
   (B) a porpoise
   (C) a sea turtle

2. Who is Timmy?
   (A) a mermaid
   (B) a porpoise
   (C) a sea turtle

3. Who is Paul?
   (A) a mermaid
   (B) a porpoise
   (C) a sea turtle

4. Who likes riding the waves?
   (A) Meredith
   (B) Paul
   (C) Timmy

Story #8

Fairyland

Andrea's grandmother gave her a magic wand for her birthday. As Andrea walked by her neighbor's garden, she spotted a fairy statue. She waved her magic wand before the statue and said, "Turn into a real fairy."

Wow! The statue turned into a real fairy. Andrea asked, "Hi, fairy. Would you like to be my friend?"

The fairy answered by winking and saying, "Yes. What should we do? I need to move around. I have been stuck in the ground as a rock statue for the past year."

"I'd like to visit Fairyland. Do you know how to get there?"

"Sure. Hold on. I'll take you there."

Off they went flying through the sky until they reached Fairyland. It was amazing. There were hundreds of fairies fluttering around in the grassy park. Some were swinging on swings, while others were riding on the backs of beautiful unicorns. The unicorns' manes and tails had all the colors of the rainbow. Andrea had never seen a unicorn before.

"You will be my friend forever," said the fairy. "I am so happy that you got me out of that garden. It was awful being a statue stuck in one place. Would you like one of my unicorn friends to take you home? You can come back and visit us whenever you want. Just call my name, Pixie, three times."

The unicorn gave Andrea a tour of Fairyland before taking her home. Andrea waved and smiled to the fairies. She couldn't wait to return to Fairyland another day.

Summarize the story in the space provided.

_____

_____

_____

_____

1. Who was the fairy?
    (A) Andrea
    (B) an imaginary friend
    (C) a statue

2. The unicorns had _____.
    (A) blue and pink manes and tails
    (B) magical powers
    (C) rainbow-colored manes and tails

3. The fairy took Andrea home.
    (A) true
    (B) false

4. How can Andrea return to Fairyland?
    (A) Just wish for it.
    (B) Say, "Pixie," three times.
    (C) She can't.

Part 1: Stories 1-16 (1 page each)

Story #9

Rescue Cat

Caitlin loves her little puppy, Coco, and her cat, Buttons. Caitlin doesn't sleep at night until they are all snuggled in together. However, Caitlin had trouble sleeping last night because Coco had gone missing. Buttons was out all night looking for him.

Just as Caitlin finished dressing in the morning, she heard Buttons at the door. Buttons was alone, but acted like he wanted Caitlin to follow him. Caitlin grabbed her coat and followed Buttons down the street. She trailed Buttons up and down a hill, through a park, and into an open field.

Caitlin thought she heard a puppy crying in the distance. The crying noises grew louder as they neared a ditch which ran alongside an open field. Buttons led Caitlin to a large pipe in the ditch. The crying noises were much louder now.

When Caitlin got closer, she could see where Coco was stuck inside the pipe. Coco's head and front legs were sticking out of the pipe, but the rest of his body was stuck.

Caitlin petted Coco's head and told him, "You will be fine. I will get you out of this mess." She gently pried his body out of the pipe. She looked him over carefully and saw that he was a little dirty, but not hurt.

Coco couldn't stop giving Caitlin and Buttons kisses. They were all very happy to be back together.

Summarize the story in the space provided.

_____

_____

_____

_____

1. Who is Coco?
   (A) Caitlin's brother
   (B) Caitlin's cat
   (C) Caitlin's puppy

2. Who is Buttons?
   (A) Caitlin's cat
   (B) Caitlin's puppy
   (C) Caitlin's sister

3. Who found the puppy?
   (A) Caitlin
   (B) Caitlin's cat
   (C) Caitlin's sister

4. What happened to the puppy?
   (A) He fell in a ditch.
   (B) He got stuck in a pipe.
   (C) Nothing happened to him.

Story #10
Star Gazer

Cassandra's nickname is Star because she is fascinated by stars. She loves the stars that you see in the night sky, not famous singers or actors.

Every clear night, Star looks up at the sky and studies the stars that she sees. She dreams about becoming an astronomer.

For her birthday, Star received a telescope. Every day when Star gets home from school, she quickly finishes her homework so that she will have more time to gaze at the stars. She really enjoys clear, moonless nights.

One evening, Star was telling her little brother, Johnny, about the Milky Way. Johnny said that he liked those kinds of candy bars. He asked if he could have one to eat.

Star doubled over laughing. "Silly boy, I'm talking about the Milky Way galaxy. Look up in the sky. It's called the Milky Way because you can see a milky band." Star pointed to the milky band in the sky. "The light that makes up the milky band comes from over one hundred billion stars. If you look through my telescope, you can see countless stars."

"Wow! That's amazing! Maybe I will get a telescope for my birthday, too."

Summarize the story in the space provided.

_____

_____

_____

_____

1. Why is Cassandra's nickname Star?
    (A) She is a great actress.
    (B) She is a great singer.
    (C) She loves astronomy.

2. Which of the following does Star like best?
    (A) clear, moonless nights
    (B) hot summer days
    (C) rainy days

3. What did Star tell Johnny about?
    (A) a candy bar
    (B) a galaxy
    (C) how to do his homework

4. There are about _____ stars are in the Milky Way.
    (A) one hundred billion
    (B) one hundred million
    (C) one hundred thousand

Story #11

Princess of the Year

My best friend's name is Carrie. I'm very proud of her. When our class voted for the princess of the year, Carrie was chosen.

Carrie is loved by everyone because she is very kind and thoughtful. If anyone around her is saying mean things about somebody, she asks them nicely to talk about something else. Carrie never gossips. I wonder if she truly is the kindest and sweetest girl in the world.

Carrie is also very helpful. She is always the first person to volunteer to help out. For example, she stays after school to help tutor classmates who need extra help.

When it was time to shop for Carrie's princess dress, she invited me to come with her and her mother. The dress she picked was light blue. The tiara she chose was silver with blue gems.

Carrie will be in the town parade. Our class will help decorate the float that she will be riding on. The float will be covered with thousands of flowers. I will help decorate the throne where she will be sitting.

Carrie has been practicing her wave for when she sits on the throne. She already has her wave perfected.

I can't wait for the day of the parade. Every student at our school will be there to cheer for her. We all know that Carrie deserves to be the princess of the year.

Summarize the story in the space provided.

_____

_____

_____

_____

1. Which statement is true?
    (A) Carrie is very helpful.
    (B) Carrie never gossips.
    (C) Both statements are true.

2. Who will see the parade?
    (A) Carrie
    (B) the teacher
    (C) the whole class

3. What color is Carrie's dress?
    (A) blue
    (B) green
    (C) pink

4. The float will be covered with _____.
    (A) flowers
    (B) gems
    (C) glitter

Part 1: Stories 1–16 (1 page each)

Story #12

Field Trip

Our class went on a field trip to the largest zoo in our state. It was a cool day so the animals were really active.

Panda cub twins were playing on a slide. They would climb up the stairs and then they would get tangled up sliding down. They were adorable. They tumbled over each other. We called them Honey and Sugar.

The monkeys were playful. They were hanging and swinging from the trees. We thought they were showing off for us. Sandi waved to them, and the monkeys waved back. We laughed hard. It also sounded like the monkeys were laughing at us. The biggest one pointed at Sandi while he laughed.

The alligators scared us. One of them came out of the water with his mouth wide open. His mouth was full of sharp teeth. Our teacher, Miss Pearson, told us that they have between seventy-four and eighty teeth. She said that their teeth get replaced when they wear down. They can go through two to three thousand teeth in a lifetime. After seeing his big mouth, we wanted to get out of there fast.

Next we saw the big cats. We saw lions, tigers, jaguars, and leopards. They were big, strong, and quick. It gave us chills when a lion stopped and looked directly at us. We all jumped backward when he suddenly roared.

When we returned to school, our teacher asked each of us to write a story about our favorite part of the field trip. It was hard to pick just one thing!

Summarize the story in the space provided.

_____

_____

_____

_____

1. What did the students call the pandas?
   (A) Salt and Honey
   (B) Sugar and Salt
   (C) Honey and Sugar

2. The students jumped when the _____.
   (A) alligator opened its mouth
   (B) largest monkey pointed at them
   (C) lion suddenly roared

3. Which animals seemed to laugh?
   (A) the lions
   (B) the monkeys
   (C) the panda bears

4. An alligator has _____ teeth.
   (A) 64 to 70
   (B) 74 to 80
   (C) 84 to 90

Story #13

Fairy Night

The stars were twinkling. The moon was full and shining brightly. Bells were ringing. Fairies and young girls were singing. It was raining pixie dust. It looked like millions of diamonds were falling from the sky. It was a magical night.

My friends and I were all dressed up in fairy costumes. The pixie dust allowed us to fly with the real fairies. Flying was the most exciting part.

Some of the fairies played violins and harps. All of us sang songs. Music was in the air.

A butterfly fairy summoned butterflies to her. The butterflies spread their beautiful wings and fluttered around us. Their wings were golden.

It was peaceful. We were happy. We laughed and giggled.

We held hands and danced in circles. Then we sat in a circle on a bed of colorful flowers. A fairy braided flowers in our hair. We wore floral tiaras. Colorful bracelets and necklaces were worn by all. We felt like real fairies.

It was an amazing night. Sweet dreams, little fairies.

Summarize the story in the space provided.

_____
_____
_____
_____

1. The girls flew with _____.
    (A) birds
    (B) fairies
    (C) stars

2. The moon was _____.
    (A) full
    (B) hidden
    (C) new

3. It was raining _____.
    (A) fairies
    (B) little diamonds
    (C) pixie dust

4. The butterflies had _____ wings.
    (A) colorful
    (B) golden
    (C) silver

Part 1: Stories 1–16 (1 page each)

Story #14

Dolphin Swim

Bethany was swimming in a lagoon when she met a mermaid named Aqua. Aqua immediately took a liking to Bethany.

Aqua asked her, "Would you like to meet my friend, Bottlenose? He is the most graceful dolphin in the whole ocean. He is also my best friend."

"Of course, I would love to meet him. Is he nearby?"

Aqua told Bethany to swim along with her. They swam past a school of beautiful butterfly fish. The coral reef was very colorful. Bethany thought it looked like a gigantic aquarium.

Aqua pointed at something in the distance. Bethany saw that it was a dolphin jumping in and out of the water.

"That's Bottlenose. He loves playing in the water."

Bottlenose swam alongside them for a while. He then motioned for Bethany to grab his fin so that he could take her for a ride. Wow! Bethany was having the time of her life. After they slowed down, Bottlenose signaled for her to climb on his back. She held on tight and enjoyed the ride. Bethany had never had so much fun in the water.

Bottlenose gave Bethany butterfly kisses when it was time for Aqua to take her back to the shore.

Summarize the story in the space provided.

_____

_____

_____

_____

1. Bethany thought that the _____ looked like a gigantic aquarium.
    (A) coral reef
    (B) mountain lake
    (C) swimming pool

2. They swam past a school of _____ fish.
    (A) butterfly
    (B) puffer
    (C) tuna

3. The mermaid's name was _____.
    (A) Aqua
    (B) Bethany
    (C) Bottlenose

4. The dolphin's name was _____.
    (A) Aqua
    (B) Bethany
    (C) Bottlenose

Part 1: Stories 1–16 (1 page each)

Story #15

Pool Party

Trisha went to a pool party to celebrate the beginning of summer. There was something for everyone to do.

There was a wading pool, a water sprinkler, a water slide, and a swimming pool. The slide had three levels. Trisha was brave and climbed to the very top the first time she went down the slide.

In the middle of the swimming pool, there was a large island in the shape of a pyramid. The kids enjoyed swimming to the island to climb the pyramid.

There were yummy party snacks, too. There were ten different flavors of snow cones. One of the kids had a special snow cone made with all ten flavors. Trisha had a cherry snow cone because it is her favorite.

Relay races and games were played all day long. Everybody won at least one prize. Trisha won a set of colorful diving sticks for holding her breath the longest underwater.

The pool party turned out to be fun for everyone. Trisha hopes to be invited again next year.

Summarize the story in the space provided.

_____

_____

_____

_____

1. The pool party was celebrating _____.
    (A) the beginning of summer
    (B) the first day of school
    (C) Trisha's birthday

2. The party was for swimmers only.
    (A) true
    (B) false

3. There were _____ snow cone flavors.
    (A) three
    (B) six
    (C) ten

4. The water slide had _____ levels.
    (A) one
    (B) two
    (C) three

Story #16

Dream Flight

The flight attendant asked Laurie, "Would you like to sit on the wing of the airplane for a better view?"

Laurie quickly answered, "Yes, please!" She didn't even know that was possible. How exciting! The flight attendant walked Laurie out onto the wing and buckled Laurie's seat belt.

As the airplane took off, Laurie loved the feel of the wind whistling by. She watched birds fly alongside the airplane.

The flight attendant was right about the view. It was beautiful from the wing. Everything looked tiny, even skyscrapers.

Laurie was enjoying the ride when she thought she felt someone tap her on the shoulder. She looked around to see a small fairy flying beside her. The fairy asked her, "Why are you sitting out here all by yourself?"

"I am sitting out here to enjoy this amazing view?"

The fairy giggled. "It would be even better if you could fly, too."

"I wish I could fly with you."

She sprinkled fairy dust over Laurie's head and said, "You now have wings and can fly with me. Unbuckle your seat belt and fly."

Laurie did as she was told. She fluttered her new wings, and began flying. She followed the fairy. Laurie waved to the surprised flight attendant. The fairy and Laurie flew to Laurie's house.

As the fairy started to fly away, she said, "I'll be back when you least expect me!" That's when Laurie woke up. The airplane had landed. Laurie was sitting on a seat inside the plane. It had all been a dream.

Summarize the story in the space provided.

_____

_____

_____

_____

1. Did Laurie really ride on the wing of an airplane?
    (A) yes
    (B) no

2. The _____ tapped Laurie on her shoulder.
    (A) fairy
    (B) flight attendant
    (C) pilot

3. Everything looked _____ from the airplane.
    (A) huge
    (B) normal
    (C) tiny

4. In the story, _____ flew alongside the airplane.
    (A) airplanes
    (B) birds
    (C) flying saucers

PART 2

Stories 17-32 (1-2 pages each)

Story #17

Rainbow Fairy

Have you seen the cutest little fairy that lives on a rainbow? She is called the Rainbow Fairy. See if you can spot her the next time you see a rainbow. She sits atop the rainbow, smiling and waving to every girl she sees.

Madison is one of the lucky girls who have met the Rainbow Fairy. When they met, Madison asked, "Rainbow Fairy, where do you go when the rainbow disappears?"

"I travel around the world. There is always a rainbow somewhere that I can sit on."

Madison wondered aloud, "Don't you ever get lonely up on the rainbow all by yourself?"

"Nope. Wherever I go, I slide down the rainbow and meet people at the bottom."

"You are talking to me in English. How do you communicate with girls in other countries? What if they only speak Spanish or French, for example?"

"My fairy godmother taught me to speak every language. She wanted me to be able to speak with every person I meet, no matter where I am."

Madison said, "You are so lucky to live on beautiful rainbows. I am sure you are loved by everyone. I bet you are never teased."

"My fairy godmother also taught me to be kind to every person in the world. She taught me how important it is to treat others how you would like to be treated. I believe that every girl is beautiful in her own way, both inside and out."

"Your fairy godmother sounds like a very special person. I am so happy that I am one of the lucky girls that could meet you."

The Rainbow Fairy smiled and said, "Thank you. I enjoyed meeting you, too. I hope to see you again someday."

The rainbow started to fade. "It looks like the rainbow is about to disappear," Madison said. "Goodbye, Rainbow Fairy. I will look for you every time I see a rainbow."

"Goodbye, Madison."

Summarize the story in the space provided.

_____

_____

_____

_____

_____

Part 2: Stories 17–32 (1–2 pages each)

1. The Rainbow Fairy believes that every girl is beautiful.
    (A) true
    (B) false

2. What language can the Rainbow Fairy speak?
    (A) English
    (B) French
    (C) Spanish
    (D) all of the above

3. When the rainbow disappears, where does the Rainbow Fairy go?
    (A) on a cloud
    (B) to another rainbow
    (C) to her house

4. Does the Rainbow Fairy ever get lonely?
    (A) yes
    (B) no

Reading Comprehension for Girls – Julie Harper

Story #18

Slumber Party

Tammy was excited when she received an invitation to a slumber party. She had never been to one before. Plus, she had never slept overnight at a friend's house. This would be a brand new experience for her.

It was more than just a slumber party. It was also a special birthday party for her friend, Anna.

Tammy was happy when her mother allowed her to accept the invitation. There would be contests for the most creative, funniest, and cutest pajamas.

Tammy's mother took her shopping for new pajamas. There were many kinds of pajamas to choose from. Tammy selected frog pajamas with matching slippers.

On the evening of the party, Tammy's mother dropped her off at the party house. Tammy felt foolish walking outside in her pajamas and slippers. She was holding her pillow, toothbrush, and a stuffed green frog. Tammy was worried that she might look silly until she entered Anna's house. Then Tammy saw that all the girls were wearing their pajamas.

Let the party begin!

The girls lined up for a parade. Anna was wearing a princess nightgown. Other pajama costumes included a bunny rabbit, teddy bear, soccer player, duck, lion, ladybug, and monkey.

Tammy hopped and said, "Ribbit. Ribbit. Croak. Croak."

Andi was roaring because she was dressed in lion pajamas.

Jennifer was snug as a bug in her ladybug pajamas.

Part 2: Stories 17–32 (1–2 pages each)

The girls went 'quackers' over Diane's duck-footed pajamas. She carried a rubber duck in each hand. Her outfit was complete with a big, orange beak.

Anna's mother and older sister were the judges. They said all the girls were wearing adorable pajamas. They couldn't decide who should win so they said that everybody won. It was a tie. Every girl received a goodie bag.

The girls watched movies on a big-screen television. After the second movie, one of the girls threw her pillow at Anna. That started a pillow fight. Feathers were flying. It seemed funny at the time. Every girl was giggling. It didn't seem as funny when Anna's mother came in. The girls apologized and cleaned up the mess.

They slept in sleeping bags on the floor. The girls shared ghost stories before falling asleep.

When it was time to leave, Tammy hugged her friends. She can't wait for another slumber party. They are fun!

Summarize the story in the space provided.

_____
_____
_____
_____
_____

1. It was _____'s birthday.
   (A) Andi
   (B) Anna
   (C) Diane
   (D) Jennifer
   (E) Tammy

2. Who won the pajama contest?
   (A) Andi
   (B) Anna
   (C) Diane
   (D) Jennifer
   (E) Tammy
   (F) Everybody

3. Who wore the lion pajamas?
   (A) Andi
   (B) Anna
   (C) Diane
   (D) Jennifer
   (E) Tammy

4. It was _____'s first slumber party.
   (A) Andi
   (B) Anna
   (C) Diane
   (D) Jennifer
   (E) Tammy

Story #19

Golden Eagle

Celine saw a big golden eagle soaring above. It was captivating to look at. It appeared to have a wingspan of about six feet. As Celine was standing there looking at it, the eagle suddenly landed next to her. To her surprise, the eagle said, "Hi. My name is Goldie. Would you like to go for a ride?"

How could Celine turn that offer down? "Of course. I would love to go for a ride!"

They soared over the beautiful valleys and rivers in Northern California. They saw the falls in Yosemite. From there they flew over majestic trees in the Redwood forest.

Goldie landed near a lake. He said, "I am really hungry. Please wait here while I catch a fish."

Celine watched Goldie soar over the lake. He must have spotted a fish because he suddenly swooped down.

As Goldie was flying back to where she sat, Celine saw that he held a big fish in his beak. She was thinking that he must be really hungry if he could eat that big fish.

Goldie landed next to Celine. He asked her, "Would you like to share my lunch with me?"

"Thanks, but I like my fish cooked."

When Goldie stopped eating, he announced that he would take the rest home to his wife. Celine held on while they soared high up a mountain. The nest was hidden high in the cliffs. Celine would never have seen the nest if Goldie hadn't taken her there. The nest was very large. It was about two feet high and six feet wide.

Goldie's wife was happy to see him. His wife was even happier to see her lunch. She was sitting on two eggs. Goldie told Celine that the eggs were already two weeks old and would hatch in another three weeks.

It was getting dark, so Goldie said that it was time to take Celine home. When she returned home, Celine thanked Goldie for the wonderful day. She enjoyed the beautiful scenery. It was really amazing to see the nest.

Summarize the story in the space provided.

_____

_____

_____

_____

_____

Part 2: Stories 17–32 (1–2 pages each)

1. How many eggs were in the nest?
    (A) one
    (B) two
    (C) three

2. Where did they fly?
    (A) Central California
    (B) Northern California
    (C) Southern California

3. Celine ate some of Goldie's lunch.
    (A) true
    (B) false

4. How long, all together, will it take for the eggs to hatch?
    (A) two weeks
    (B) five weeks
    (C) seven weeks

Story #20

Sweet Land

Have you ever been to Sweet Land? It is the sweetest place on earth. I thought I must be dreaming because everything tastes so sweet. Oh, what a very yummy place!

Gingerbread girls and boys greet you in front of their gingerbread houses. The gingerbread houses are complete with graham crackers and frosting.

The big puffy clouds are made of white cotton candy. When it rains, sugar sprinkles fall from the sky. It snows marshmallows, which are used to make tasty snowmen.

Trees have chocolate bark and spearmint leaves. Pebbles and stones are made from mango and blackberry jelly beans. There are fields of candy corn.

The streets are lined with stores that have their own special kinds of treats. Flower shops are filled with lollipop and fluffy marshmallow flowers. Bakeries are covered with yummy chocolates, cakes, and cupcakes. The cakes are decorated with whipped cream and topped with colorful sprinkles. Inside you'll find cinnamon rolls, fresh baked muffins, and moist croissants.

Pathways of gumdrops lead to the candy store. Open the doors and you will find chocolate-covered cherries, peanut butter wafers, saltwater taffy, milk chocolate, and peanuts.

Enter a café with tables made of caramel-filled chocolate bars and chairs made of roasted peanuts covered in honey, where you can enjoy a cup of hot chocolate. You can even eat the furniture.

Part 2: Stories 17–32 (1–2 pages each)

Follow the colored jelly beans that lead to the ice-cream parlor. Wafer ice-cream cones are filled with ice-cream. Serve yourself! You'll find chocolate, vanilla, chocolate chip, rocky road, mint chocolate chip, pralines 'n cream, strawberry, lemon custard, and every other delicious flavor you can think of.

Have a seat on a cream puff while you enjoy your favorite yummy dessert.

If you haven't found Sweet Land, follow the sweet aroma of candy, cakes, and pastries, and it will surely lead you to the land of your dreams.

Summarize the story in the space provided.

_____

_____

_____

_____

1. According to the story, what is Sweet Land?
    (A) a game that children play
    (B) a place made out of sweets
    (C) stores that sell sweets

2. When it rains, _____ fall from the sky.
    (A) cotton candy
    (B) marshmallows
    (C) sugar sprinkles

3. _____ greet you when you enter Sweet Land.
    (A) Gingerbread girls and boys
    (B) Ice-cream parlors
    (C) Marshmallow snowmen

4. Pathways of gumdrops lead to the _____.
    (A) bakery
    (B) candy store
    (C) ice-cream parlor

Part 2: Stories 17–32 (1–2 pages each)

Story #21

Mermaid Friend

One day, Stephanie was swimming in her favorite lagoon when she spotted a mermaid. Stephanie swam up close to the mermaid and said, "Hi, pretty mermaid. May I swim with you?"

"I would love that," replied the mermaid. "Sometimes I get lonely. Although I have many friends in the sea, I only have a few girlfriends to hang out with."

"Oh, miss mermaid, I would love to be your friend."

They swam around in the lagoon. The mermaid pointed out sea creatures that Stephanie had never noticed before. They saw sea urchins, sea cucumbers, sand dollars, and starfish.

The mermaid warned Stephanie to stay away from the puffer fish because they have very sharp spines. The mermaid said that they are poisonous if touched, and that a puffer fish can expand its body when faced with danger.

They visited a sandy beach where they saw several crabs. Two of the crabs were arguing. The mermaid complained how silly it was that the crabs argue most of the time. The crabs' names were Crabby and Cranky.

The mermaid suggested that Crabby and Cranky settle their argument with a friendly race. The crabs agreed to race. The first crab to climb up to the top of the rocks and back to where they started would be the winner.

The race was on! The race looked odd to Stephanie because the crabs walked sideways, and not in a straight line. The faster they went, the more they walked sideways. It was a close race as they started up the pile of rocks. Crabby was the first to reach the top, but Cranky was close behind him. They headed back down the rocks. Cranky found a long smooth rock that he slid down. Now he was next to Crabby. They headed to the finish line.

It was a tie! Neither one of them won. They went right back to arguing. The mermaid said, "I tried my best to get you two to stop arguing, but I guess it's not going to happen. Stephanie and I are going to leave you two alone."

Stephanie said, "I can't believe that you have crabs for friends. I hope you will always be my friend."

"Please come and swim with me any time you can."

Summarize the story in the space provided.

_____
_____
_____
_____
_____

Part 2: Stories 17–32 (1–2 pages each)

1. Who won the crab race?
    (A) Crabby
    (B) Cranky
    (C) Neither. It was a tie.

2. Why did the crabs run a race?
    (A) to get some exercise
    (B) to settle an argument
    (C) to win a gold medal

3. The mermaid said not to touch the _____.
    (A) puffer fish
    (B) sand dollar
    (C) sea cucumber
    (D) sea urchin
    (E) starfish

4. The mermaid had only a few _____.
    (A) girlfriends
    (B) sand dollars
    (C) sea friends

Story #22

Robot Design

Our teacher gave us a special homework assignment: If we could program a robot to do anything, what would it be?

The most popular answer was, "Do my homework for me." The second most popular response was, "Do my chores."

Katie's idea won second place. She would like to have a flying robot to take her wherever she goes. She wouldn't need to take the bus to school. Her ride would be waiting for her when the bell rings. She would just hop on the robot, and the robot would fly her to her home.

The robot could take her to the movies, the mall, or her friend's house. Katie's classmates thought it was a neat idea. Katie's robot would be like a personalized taxi. Katie said that she would let her friends take rides, too.

Sally had the most creative answer. She won first place. Sally said that she would program her robot to teach her little brother good manners. Sally went into detail telling us exactly what the robot would do.

Sally said that the robot would calm her brother down whenever he started yelling. The robot would prevent him from cutting into his sister's conversations. He would wait patiently until their conversation ended. He would respect his sister's personal space. When Sally's friends are visiting, he wouldn't follow them around, prying into everything they do. The robot would also teach him to use the words "please" and "thank you."

Part 2: Stories 17–32 (1–2 pages each)

All the girls in our class who have little brothers told Sally that her idea was pure genius. We all want her robot! The boys weren't too thrilled about the idea, though.

Summarize the story in the space provided.

_____
_____
_____
_____
_____

1. Which was the most popular answer?
    (A) The robot would be a taxi.
    (B) The robot would do chores.
    (C) The robot would do homework.
    (D) The robot would teach good manners.

2. Which was the second most popular answer?
    (A) The robot would be a taxi.
    (B) The robot would do chores.
    (C) The robot would do homework.
    (D) The robot would teach good manners.

3. Which answer won first place?
    (A) The robot would be a taxi.
    (B) The robot would do chores.
    (C) The robot would do homework.
    (D) The robot would teach good manners.

4. Which answer won second place?
    (A) The robot would be a taxi.
    (B) The robot would do chores.
    (C) The robot would do homework.
    (D) The robot would teach good manners.

Story #23

Birthday Surprise

It happened on Tuesday on my way home from school. My poodle, named Curly, met me about a block from my home. She had a surprise for me. A bright pink ribbon was loosely tied around her neck. An envelope with my name on it was tied to the ribbon. I quickly opened the envelope and read the letter:

> Dear Kaylee,
>
> Today is your birthday. When you get home, look under the doormat. You will find a magic key that opens the door to the birthday castle. A carriage will be there at 4:00 p.m. to take you and your best friend, Emma, to the castle.
>
> Happy birthday! Have fun.
>
> Love,
>
> Mom & Dad

I called Emma right away. Then I went to my dressing room. I wanted to look nice for my birthday party.

Sure enough, at 4:00 p.m. sharp the carriage was in front of my house. When Emma and I arrived at the castle, there was a sign on the door:

> If you use the magic key to unlock this door, you will magically turn into a princess as you enter the castle.

I eagerly unlocked the door. We entered a mirrored room. What we saw was breathtaking. Emma and I were both dressed in beautiful gowns and were wearing jeweled tiaras. My gown was my favorite color—pink. Emma wore a bright blue gown that matched her sparkling eyes.

A prince walked in singing a happy birthday song to me. Emma sang along, too.

The prince led us to the ballroom. He proved to be a gentleman and a good dancing partner. The prince never seemed to tire. He danced with us until our feet hurt.

We worked up a good appetite. It was time for birthday cake and ice-cream. The cake was in the shape of a castle. It tasted just as delicious as it looked.

The prince asked us to take the leftover cake home so that we could share it with our families.

The birthday celebration had come to an end. The carriage was waiting to take us home. The prince kissed each of us on the cheek and wished me a very happy birthday. I will never forget that birthday party.

Part 2: Stories 17–32 (1–2 pages each)

Summarize the story in the space provided.

_____

_____

_____

_____

_____

1. The poodle was carrying a _____.
    (A) cake
    (B) key
    (C) note

2. What is Kaylee's favorite color?
    (A) blue
    (B) pink
    (C) yellow

3. The cake was shaped like a _____.
    (A) carriage
    (B) castle
    (C) princess

4. What color are Emma's eyes?
    (A) blue
    (B) brown
    (C) green

Story #24

Harsh Words

Catherine is very beautiful. I think that she looks and dresses just like a real princess would.

One day, at lunchtime, I had a chance to talk to Catherine. I told her how beautiful she looks. I thought she would be happy to hear that, but what she did next came as a shock.

She told me that I looked like an ugly ogre. I wasn't sure what an ogre was, but I knew what ugly meant.

I was very sad that afternoon at school. I cried in my bed when I got home. My older sister, Sissy, knocked on my bedroom door. I didn't answer. She came in anyway.

She asked, "Missy, what's wrong?"

I continued crying for a while. Then I told her, "Catherine told me that I look like an ugly ogre."

"Oh, Missy, you are not ugly. You are beautiful inside and outside. Can't you see it? Catherine is very beautiful on the outside, but very unsure of herself. Sometimes insecure girls criticize others because they think it makes them look better."

Sissy gave me the best advice. She said, "Be confident. Smile when you see her. Don't let her get you down. When it's just the two of you, tell her that what she said to you was mean."

Sissy held up a mirror so that I could see myself. She wiped the tears from my eyes. She told me a joke. Then she said, "Do you see that? It's a beautiful smile."

Part 2: Stories 17–32 (1–2 pages each)

The next day, I saw Catherine in the school hallway. I approached her and asked her why she had said such a mean thing to me. She was surprised when I confronted her. She said that she was truly sorry, and didn't really mean to hurt me. We talked for a long time.

Catherine said that she didn't realize how many mean things she had been saying to other girls. She asked me to let her know when she says something that isn't nice. Every week, she gets better at being nice. She is learning to be more confident in herself, too.

Catherine now has several friends, including me. Now she is truly beautiful on the inside as well as the outside.

I am glad that I talked to her. I feel much better now, and I know that Catherine is happier too.

Summarize the story in the space provided.

_____

_____

_____

_____

_____

1. What made Missy cry?
   (A) She failed a test.
   (B) She twisted her ankle.
   (C) Someone called her ugly.

2. Missy received good advice from _____.
   (A) Catherine
   (B) her father
   (C) her mother
   (D) her sister
   (E) her teacher

3. What advice did Missy receive?
   (A) She should talk to Catherine about the problem.
   (B) She shouldn't believe that she really is ugly.
   (C) Some girls say mean things to feel better about themselves.
   (D) All of the above.

4. Missy and Catherine are now friends.
   (A) true
   (B) false

Story #25

Best Friend

Rosa is the best friend a girl could ever have. She never says anything hurtful, even if someone else has said something hurtful to her. Rosa is also the type of girl who stands up for her friends.

Maggie is one of Rosa's best friends. Maggie is pretty sure that Rosa always thinks before she speaks. Maggie asked Rosa about it one day.

Rosa said, "Maggie, I've always wanted to be a princess. I know that a princess isn't just a pretty girl. In fact, it's more important to be beautiful from within. I try to remember to think before I speak so that I can be beautiful on the inside. I believe it's what a true princess would do."

One day, Maggie and Rosa were eating lunch with two other girls, Olivia and Joanna. Olivia told Joanna, "Your dress looks like something that your mother would wear." Joanna promptly grabbed her lunch and left.

Rosa turned to Olivia and asked, "You didn't really mean what you said. Did you?"

Olivia answered, "Don't you think it looks like something her mother would wear?"

"No. I don't think it does. Joanna can wear what she wants. You shouldn't criticize her for what she chooses to wear."

"Whoa! I didn't mean to hurt anyone. I just think her dress doesn't look like something a young girl would wear."

"Maybe you should think before you speak, Olivia. What you told Joanna is very hurtful."

Olivia said, "I will go apologize to Joanna. I didn't realize I was being mean. Now I know why everyone likes you, Rosa. You really care about the feelings of your friends."

"Yes. I do care about my friends. I also care about the feelings of people I don't even know. I would like you to be my friend, too."

"That would be so nice," Olivia answered. "I will try to be like you. I don't want to hurt anyone. I really want the other girls to like me."

Rosa said, "Let's start by you apologizing to Joanna. Just remember, when you apologize it must come from your heart. An apology doesn't mean anything unless you're sincere."

"I will do my best to be her friend, and yours, too."

Summarize the story in the space provided.

_____
_____
_____
_____
_____

Part 2: Stories 17–32 (1–2 pages each)

1. Who said something hurtful?
    (A) Maggie
    (B) Joanna
    (C) Olivia
    (D) Rosa

2. Who stood up for someone else?
    (A) Maggie
    (B) Joanna
    (C) Olivia
    (D) Rosa

3. Promptly means _____.
    (A) done loudly
    (B) done quickly
    (C) done quietly
    (D) done slowly
    (E) not done at all

4. A princess is just a pretty girl.
    (A) true
    (B) false

Story #26

Water Park

One hot summer afternoon, a group of friends met at the local water park.

They cooled off under the misters while they decided which ride they wanted to go on first. Sheri and Vanessa wanted to go on the tallest and fastest water slide. It's called the Bottomless Pit. It isn't really bottomless, but it has a long, dark tunnel.

Sam, Monica, and Tina didn't want to ride the Bottomless Pit. They were already frightened just from looking at it.

Sam had an idea. She said, "Why don't we start out with some of the calmer rides? Then we can work our way up to the scary rides, like the Bottomless Pit."

Monica and Tina said that Sam's suggestion was splendid. Sheri and Vanessa really wanted to go down the Bottomless Pit slide, but agreed that Sam's idea was a good compromise.

They first went on some friendly water slides. Then they rode on a raft together that twisted and turned through whitewater rapids. They got soaked when the raft went under a waterfall.

When the time came to ride the Bottomless Pit, the girls climbed the stairs. When they reached the top, Sam was frightened just looking down.

Sam was practically crying when she said, "There is no way that I can go down that slide. I will meet you at the bottom." Monica and Tina agreed with Sam that it was too scary.

Part 2: Stories 17–32 (1–2 pages each)

Sam, Monica, and Tina took the elevator down to the bottom. Then they waited for Sheri and Vanessa to come down the slide. They could hear their friends screaming before they could see them. When Sheri and Vanessa got off the ride, all the girls started giggling. They continued giggling for several minutes. They didn't know who had more fun: the riders or the watchers.

Sam, Monica, and Tina whispered to one another.

"Hey, girls! No secrets!" Sheri and Vanessa teased in unison.

"Okay," Sam answered. "After seeing how much fun you had, we want to go on it with you. Are you ready to go down the Bottomless Pit slide again?"

This time, all five girls went on the slide. They all screamed on the way down, yet everyone had fun. Sam, Monica, and Tina were glad that they tried it, and Sheri and Vanessa were happy about it, also.

Summarize the story in the space provided.

_____
_____
_____
_____
_____

1. Which girls were afraid of the Bottomless Pit?
Select all that apply.
    (A) Monica
    (B) Sam
    (C) Sheri
    (D) Tina
    (E) Vanessa

2. Which girls wanted to ride the Bottomless Pit first?
Select all that apply.
    (A) Monica
    (B) Sam
    (C) Sheri
    (D) Tina
    (E) Vanessa

3. The Bottomless Pit didn't have a bottom.
    (A) true
    (B) false

4. All five girls eventually went down the Bottomless Pit.
    (A) true
    (B) false

Part 2: Stories 17–32 (1–2 pages each)

Story #27

Royal Feast

The prince knows how important a good education is. He reviews the report cards of every student in his kingdom. Every year, the top two students are invited to his castle.

This year, Reese and Jordan had the top marks. The prince was impressed with their nearly perfect report cards. He wanted to reward them for achieving such excellent grades.

A golden carriage arrived at the school to pick up Reese and Jordan. Four beautiful white horses pulled the carriage. Their manes and tails were braided with gold ribbons. The prince sat between the two girls. He treated them like royalty.

When they arrived at the castle, the guards saluted them. The king's guards had planned a parade on their behalf. The prince and the girls were escorted to stands where they had front-row seats. The guards were dressed in their finest uniforms. It was fun to watch, and quite an honor for Reese and Jordan.

After the parade, the prince personally gave the girls a tour of the castle. They had never seen such luxury. Everything was polished and sparkling. All of the rooms were decorated with lavish furniture.

A royal feast was held in the girls' honor. They sat at the main table with the prince, princess, queen, and king. The girls were treated like family. The china and crystal were elegant. The food was plentiful and delicious. Reese and Jordan enjoyed every bite.

After dinner, the girls were taken to the ballroom. It was decorated in their favorite colors. They were in the spotlight when the prince asked them for the first dance. It was very exciting for them to dance with the prince.

The wonderful day ended with the prince giving a speech to honor the two girls. The prince gave the girls each a beautiful tiara as a keepsake.

Reese and Jordan were proud to be the guests of honor. It was the most extraordinary day of their lives. They will enjoy this day forever. They will also tell their classmates all about it. Their classmates will work very hard next year, hoping to earn this special honor.

Summarize the story in the space provided.

_____

_____

_____

_____

_____

Part 2: Stories 17–32 (1–2 pages each)

1. Why were Reese and Jordan invited to the castle?
    (A) They had the best grades.
    (B) They were related to the prince.
    (C) They won a lottery.

2. How did Reese and Jordan get to the castle?
    (A) golden carriage
    (B) school bus
    (C) they walked

3. The prince danced with Reese and Jordan.
    (A) true
    (B) false

4. Each girl received a _____ as a keepsake.
    (A) crystal
    (B) tiara
    (C) trophy

Story #28

Magic Bike

This was the first time that Charlene rode her bike to school.

Charlene pedaled her bike faster and faster until she was pedaling as fast as she could. She picked up so much speed that it started to lift up off the ground. Up it went. It was flying! Charlene and her bike were up in the sky, looking down at the cars and houses.

When Charlene approached the school, one of the students saw her. He pointed and yelled, "Hey, everybody, look at that!"

The other students looked up in the sky. They were all shocked to see a girl flying a bike in the air. They stopped what they were doing, and just stared. When Charlene landed, all the students came running up to her.

The other students were all talking at the same time. One asked, "Charlene, how can your bike fly?"

Another inquired, "Where did you get it?"

"Can I have a ride?"

As Charlene walked her bike to the bike rack to lock it, she answered, "It's my magic bike. No one else has ever had a bike like this."

All day long, the other students couldn't think of anything else. They talked about Charlene and her magic bike. They wondered how they could get bikes like the one Charlene had.

When the bell rang at three o'clock, Charlene told her best friend, June, that she would give her a ride. When they hopped on the bike, Charlene told June, "Hold on. I have a surprise for you."

Part 2: Stories 17–32 (1–2 pages each)

June couldn't imagine being more surprised than she already was. After all, seeing a bike fly is pretty amazing.

Charlene pedaled faster and faster until the bike, Charlene, and June rose up into the sky. The bike went over their houses and kept on flying.

Soon, June recognized the home of her godmother. June hadn't seen her for months. Wow! That was a surprise.

After they landed in the driveway, Charlene said, "I know that your godmother is sick and that you haven't been able to see her lately. I brought you here so that you could see her."

"Oh, thank you. What a wonderful surprise! Let's go inside and see her."

June's godmother was very happy to see them. She was feeling better, too. June's godmother happily served cookies and punch. She always has June's favorite chocolate chip cookies on-hand, just in case.

June told her godmother about Charlene's magic bike.

Charlene said, "I can bring June here once a week to see you." June and her godmother were happy to hear that.

Summarize the story in the space provided.

_____
_____
_____
_____

1. Which of these titles best fits this story?
    (A) June Has Magic Powers
    (B) June Has a Magic Bike
    (C) Charlene Has Magic Powers
    (D) Charlene Has a Magic Bike

2. What was special about the bike?
    (A) It could fly.
    (B) It didn't have pedals.
    (C) It went very fast.

3. What was June's surprise?
    (A) She received a magic bike.
    (B) She saw her godmother.
    (C) She visited a castle.

4. Charlene and June will return to see June's godmother once every _____.
    (A) day
    (B) week
    (C) month
    (D) year

Part 2: Stories 17–32 (1–2 pages each)

Story #29

Camping Scare

Julie's family went on a camping trip. Julie's parents told her that she could bring her best friend, Alexis. Julie's little brother, Phil, was also bringing his friend, Roger. Julie hoped that Phil and Roger wouldn't follow her around and bug her like they usually do.

When they arrived at the campsite, Julie and Alexis had fun setting up the girls' tent. The boys didn't bother them because they had gone fishing.

The air was chilly when the sun set. Julie's dad started a campfire. After the others settled in for the night, Julie and Alexis stayed around the campfire. They had fun telling each other spooky stories.

The girls heard a noise. It sounded like twigs snapping. They looked at each other with fear in their eyes. Julie whispered, "Did you hear that? What could it be?"

"Maybe it's Bigfoot," replied Alexis. "I heard that he has been seen in this part of the woods."

Oh, no! The girls could see bushes moving and heard more twigs snapping. They both jumped up and screamed. They held each other tightly. Julie whispered, "Maybe if we sit here quietly, it will go away."

They didn't hear anything except for crackling noises from the campfire. Julie and Alexis relaxed. Maybe it did go away. Alexis said, "We probably just scared ourselves telling spooky stories."

The girls decided to make themselves some s'mores. They were enjoying the s'mores when they heard more twigs snapping. Then they heard a different noise, sort of like moaning.

Julie and Alexis both asked, "Who's there?"

No one answered.

Alexis whispered in Julie's ear, "Let's jump up at the same time and scream as loud as we can. Maybe we can scare it away."

The girls suddenly jumped high in the air and screamed at the top of their lungs.

Two figures screamed and ran into the campsite. It was Phil and Roger. The boys were afraid for their lives.

The girls were laughing hard. The boys were trying to scare the girls, but the girls wound up scaring the boys.

Summarize the story in the space provided.

_____

_____

_____

_____

_____

Part 2: Stories 17-32 (1-2 pages each)

1. What did Julie's dad do to keep the campers warm?
    (A) He lit a barbecue.
    (B) He started a campfire.
    (C) He turned on the heater.

2. Who was scaring the girls?
    (A) Bigfoot
    (B) Julie's parents
    (C) Phil and Roger

3. What did the girls eat?
    (A) hot dogs
    (B) popcorn
    (C) s'mores

4. The boys wound up being the ones who were scared.
    (A) true
    (B) false

Story #30

Fashion Design

Claudia only has one dress to wear. Don't start feeling sorry for her. She is very fashionable. You ask how that can be? Well, the one dress she has is a magic dress. What is a magic dress? This story will show you.

When Claudia dressed for school this morning, her dress was a bright pink sundress. She isn't allowed to wear a sundress to school. She needed a uniform instead. When Claudia arrived at the school, she rubbed the sundress and said, "Turn into a blue and khaki school dress uniform." Her sundress magically turned into a school uniform.

When Claudia returned home from school, her mom told her to get ready for her dance class. Claudia rubbed her uniform, and said, "Change into a blue tutu." As amazing as it seems, Claudia was suddenly wearing a cute tutu outfit.

After dance class, Claudia had a birthday party to attend. Her best friend, Sandi, was having a birthday.

Sandi always wears trendy clothes because her mother is a fashion designer. Claudia wanted to look nice for Sandi's party. She rubbed the tutu and said, "Turn into a fancy party dress." The tutu turned into the dress of Claudia's dreams. It was perfect for her party dress.

The party was fun. There was a fashion parade. All the girls modeled their dresses. Sandi, the birthday girl, led the parade. The girls enjoyed showing off their pretty dresses. Sandi's mother was impressed with Claudia's fancy dress.

Part 2: Stories 17–32 (1–2 pages each)

Claudia forgot that the party was a sleepover. She didn't bring her pajamas. Nobody knew about her magic dress, and she wanted to keep it a secret. She quietly slipped into the bathroom. She rubbed her party dress and said, "Change into a pajama gown." Her party dress turned into a cute, frilly pajama gown. Claudia wondered what she would have done if she didn't have the magic dress with her.

Claudia thinks she is the luckiest girl to have this one magic dress. It's like having a million dresses in one.

Wouldn't it be wonderful if every young girl in the world had her own magic dress?

Summarize the story in the space provided.

_____

_____

_____

_____

_____

1. What was special about the magic dress?
    (A) It brought good luck.
    (B) It could do her homework.
    (C) It was like having a million dresses in one.

2. Claudia forgot to bring _____ to the party.
    (A) a cake
    (B) a card
    (C) a gift
    (D) pajamas

3. Who is a fashion designer?
    (A) Claudia
    (B) Claudia's mother
    (C) Sandi
    (D) Sandi's mother

4. Claudia shared the secret about her magic dress.
    (A) true
    (B) false

Story #31

Magic Time

Our teacher, Miss Winters, showed us a clock. It looked like the one hanging in our classroom, but it turned out to be very different from an ordinary clock.

Miss Winters explained, "This isn't just an ordinary clock. If you set the time on the clock, it will suddenly be that time of the day for you. For example, if you don't wish to wait for lunch, set the clock to 12:30 p.m. It will suddenly be lunchtime for you. However, you can only skip forward; you can't go back in time. I will let each of you check the clock out for one day."

Kim was the first student to check out the clock. When Kim woke up in the morning, she set the clock to 3:00 p.m. This way, Kim didn't need to go to school that day. Kim walked over to the school bus stop to meet her friend, Karen, coming home from school. Kim asked Karen, "How was school today?"

Karen answered, "It was great. We took a field trip to the cookie factory. They showed us how they make and package cookies. They gave us samples of all the different kinds of cookies. It was a fun day!"

"Oh no, I forgot all about that! What a fool I was for setting the clock for 3:00 p.m. All I was thinking about was the chance to skip school. I wish I had remembered the field trip."

The next day, April had the clock. April adjusted the clock to 10:30 a.m. That's when her art class begins. Since April loves art, she wanted her school day to start with art class. Using the clock, April was able to begin her day by painting her self-portrait.

On the third day, Billy checked out the clock. It was Billy's birthday. He set the clock for 4:00 p.m. because that was the time when his birthday party started. Billy didn't need to wait all day for his party to begin.

Maryann was the next student to check out the clock. It was Friday night. Maryann adjusted the clock to 6:00 a.m. Saturday morning. Her dad was surprised to see Maryann up early on a Saturday morning. Maryann explained that she wanted to enjoy the full day. Since Maryann was up early, her dad was able to spend time with her before he did his Saturday chores. He took her to breakfast, and then they went shopping. Maryann couldn't remember ever spending so much time with her dad before. He was usually very busy working.

After all of the students had a chance to check out the clock, Miss Winters asked us to share our experiences. We had fun sharing what we had done.

Summarize the story in the space provided.

_____
_____
_____
_____
_____

Part 2: Stories 17–32 (1–2 pages each)

1. What happened when Kim used the clock to skip school?
    (A) She ate breakfast with her dad and went shopping.
    (B) She finished painting her self-portrait.
    (C) She missed a field trip to a cookie factory.
    (D) She was arrested by a truant officer.
    (E) She went to a birthday party.

2. Why did April set the clock for 10:30 a.m.?
    (A) to eat breakfast with her father
    (B) to finish painting her self-portrait
    (C) to get ready for a birthday party
    (D) to go to the cookie factory
    (E) to skip her art class

3. Why did Billy set the clock for 4:00 p.m.?
    (A) to eat breakfast with his father
    (B) to finish painting his self-portrait
    (C) to get ready for a birthday party
    (D) to go to the cookie factory
    (E) to skip his art class

4. What happened when Maryann set the clock for 6:00 a.m.?
    (A) She ate breakfast with her dad and went shopping.
    (B) She finished painting her self-portrait.
    (C) She missed a field trip to a cookie factory.
    (D) She was arrested by a truant officer.
    (E) She went to a birthday party.

Story #32

Special Glasses

Carolina has a special pair of glasses. They look like regular eyeglasses, but they are far from normal. When Carolina wears her special glasses, she can see things that other people can't.

One day, Carolina saw a little girl who looked very sad. Carolina asked her, "What's wrong? Why are you so sad?"

The little girl was sobbing so hard that she could hardly answer. Between sobs she said, "I lost my puppy."

Carolina said, "Don't worry, little girl. I can find your puppy. What's your name?"

"Sonya. Can you really find him?"

"You bet. What does he look like? What's his name?"

"His name is Toby. He's a little black and white shih tzu. Please… please find him for me."

As Carolina walked through the town, she closely watched every person she saw. After a while, she saw something in the eyes of a young boy. Using her special glasses, she could tell that he had seen the puppy recently. She asked the boy, "Where did you see the little black and white puppy?"

The boy answered, "How do you know that I saw the puppy?"

Carolina said, "I can see it in your eyes. Please tell me. Where did you last see him?"

"He was in the sandbox at the park."

Carolina ran as fast as she could to the park. Toby was no longer there. She saw his footprints in the sand. Her special glasses showed her that the dog had gone to a nearby factory.

Part 2: Stories 17–32 (1–2 pages each)

Carolina went to the factory. Once there, she stopped and looked around. Her special glasses helped her see inside containers and to look through walls. She saw Toby sleeping inside of a large crate.

Toby must have crawled through a hole in the side of the crate. Carolina was too big to fit through the hole. She looked around with her special glasses. Through the wall of the building, she saw a guard sitting inside.

Carolina knocked on the door. When the guard answered, she asked, "Could you please get the puppy out of the crate?"

The guard wondered how she knew there was a puppy in a crate, but quickly helped rescue the puppy.

Toby woke up and looked happy. He licked Carolina's face when she picked him up. Carolina brought the puppy to Sonya. The little girl had a big smile on her face when she saw Toby.

Summarize the story in the space provided.

_____
_____
_____
_____

1. A shih tzu is a _____.

   (A) girl who rescues animals

   (B) little black and white dog

   (C) man who guards a factory

   (D) park that has a sandbox

   (E) special pair of glasses

2. Carolina wears glasses _____.

   (A) so that it won't look too bright outside

   (B) to change her eye color

   (C) to improve her eyesight

   (D) to see in black and white

   (E) to see things that other people can't

3. Sonya was sad because she _____.

   (A) lost her glasses

   (B) lost her puppy

   (C) lost her purse

   (D) was late for school

   (E) was lost

4. The puppy licked _____'s face.

   (A) Carolina

   (B) Sonya

   (C) the boy

   (D) the guard

   (E) Toby

PART 3

Stories 33-48 (2-3 pages each)

Part 3: Stories 33–48 (2–3 pages each)

Story #33

Mrs. Crabtree

Mrs. Crabtree lives three houses down from us. The kids in our neighborhood think that her name suits her just fine. She is always crabby, and never smiles or says, "Hello." When a ball lands in her yard, she keeps it. She yells at us if she thinks we are making too much noise. Every kid in the neighborhood knows this.

When kids are walking down the sidewalk, they cross the street to avoid walking in front of Mrs. Crabtree's house.

That's what I usually do, too, but I was in a hurry to get home this afternoon. Instead of crossing the street, I figured that I could dash past her house without being seen. Boy, was I wrong!

I heard Mrs. Crabtree call out to me, "Amy, stop. I need to speak with you."

As I continued walking past her house, I said quietly, "But, but… I'm in a hurry to get home."

"Amy, it will only take a few minutes of your time."

I looked around to see if any of my friends were watching. I didn't see anyone, so I followed Mrs. Crabtree to her backyard.

When we got there, I couldn't believe my eyes. Five fairies were swinging from flowering trees. Three more fairies were swimming in her pool.

"Wow! Mrs. Crabtree, I didn't know you had fairies in your backyard. Do they live with you? How is it possible?"

Before Mrs. Crabtree could answer, the fairies came over to us and started singing a happy birthday song—to me!

"Amy, your mother told me that today is your birthday. The fairies love birthday parties, so I was hoping that you would come over to visit."

One of the fairies braided my hair with ribbons and flowers in my favorite color—yellow. Another fairy painted my fingernails and toenails with a sparkly polish that matched the ribbons. They also gave me a beautiful yellow tutu. Mrs. Crabtree put a birthday tiara in my hair.

Three fairies brought birthday presents to me. The gifts were jeweled rings, necklaces, and bracelets.

We ate a frosted birthday cake that was shaped like a castle.

"Oh, how can I ever thank you? This is wonderful!"

"I would love for you and your friends to stop and visit with me. I don't know why all of you kids never say hello or smile."

"But, Mrs. Crabtree, everybody knows that you never smile, you keep a ball if it comes into your yard, and you yell at us if we make too much noise."

Mrs. Crabtree smiled and asked, "Have you ever seen me keep a ball? Have you ever heard me yell?"

"Well, um… No, not really."

Tears were rolling down Mrs. Crabtree's cheeks. "A few kids started rumors about me many years ago. They said that I don't like children. That's not true. The truth is that I'm lonely and would love to share my fairies with you and your friends."

Now I was crying. "I was wrong to have believed what I heard. I am so sorry. I will always be your friend. I will tell everyone I know how nice you really are. Mrs. Crabtree, thanks for giving me the best birthday ever!"

"You are welcome, birthday girl."

Part 3: Stories 33–48 (2–3 pages each)

1. Why did Mrs. Crabtree ask Amy to stop?
    (A) Amy was making too much noise.
    (B) Amy was running too fast.
    (C) She had a surprise for Amy.
    (D) She wanted to return Amy's ball.
    (E) She wanted to scare Amy.

2. What is Amy's favorite color?
    (A) blue
    (B) green
    (C) pink
    (D) purple
    (E) yellow

3. What did Amy find in Mrs. Crabtree's backyard?
    (A) balls
    (B) birds
    (C) butterflies
    (D) fairies
    (E) fireflies

4. Mrs. Crabtree really is mean.
    (A) true
    (B) false

Story #34

Island Magic

On a sunny afternoon in July, Janie and Karla were playing in the ocean waves. A sea turtle swam up to them. To their surprise, the sea turtle spoke. He asked the girls if they would like a ride to a magical island.

Janie asked, "What's magical about it?"

"There are beautiful shells and sea jewels. Some of the gems bring good luck. You might even get to swim with one of the mermaids. Many mermaids live near the island."

Janie and Karla both answered at the same time. "Yes. Please take us to the magical island. It sounds like fun."

"Hop on! My name is Tommy. I know that each of you will have a super day."

Both girls climbed onto Tommy's shell. Tommy swam toward a distant island. When they passed a sea lion, Tommy nodded and said, "Hello." The sea lion waved a fin, and then swam alongside them for a while. The sea lion was noisy. The girls thought it was cute how he frequently stuck his head out of the water and made a barking sound.

As they neared the magical island, Tommy pointed to a beautiful green and blue mermaid named Pearl. Tommy waved to Pearl and said, "My new friends would like to swim with you today. Please meet them at the island later this afternoon."

When they reached the island, Tommy dropped Janie and Karla off. He said, "Have fun. I will pick you up about an hour before sunset."

Part 3: Stories 33–48 (2–3 pages each)

Janie and Karla explored the island. They discovered a cove and found a treasure chest there. When they opened the chest, there was a map inside. The map led them to an X drawn in the sand. They dug in the sand and found jeweled necklaces and bracelets. They soon wore several necklaces around their necks and bracelets on their wrists.

Janie and Karla giggled while chasing one another around the island. After a while, Janie said, "Let's go swimming." While they were swimming, Janie spotted Pearl.

They swam alongside the mermaid. Pearl motioned for the girls to follow her. Pearl led them to a coral reef garden. There were schools of colorful fish swimming in the coral reef. Janie thought it looked like a gigantic aquarium.

Next, Pearl brought the girls to an underwater rock formation. There they found starfish in a variety of colors and sizes.

Janie and Karla were tired, so they decided to rest and sunbathe on the sandy beach. A while later, Janie said, "Pearl, Tommy mentioned gems that bring good luck. Do you know where we can find them?"

Pearl answered, "I see from the necklaces and bracelets that you're wearing that you found the treasure chest and followed the map. There are some star-shaped gems where you found the buried jewels. People believe that the bright red gems bring good luck. Let's go there. I will help you look for them."

They returned to where Janie and Karla had found their buried jewelry. Janie, Karla, and Pearl dug in the sand. Pearl announced, "I found two of the lucky gems." Pearl handed one to each of the girls.

"Wow! They are beautiful," said Karla.

Janie asked, "Can we keep them?"

"Take them home and carry them with you wherever you go. Please bury the necklaces and bracelets that you don't need so that other girls may find them." Janie and Karla each kept one bracelet, one necklace, and one lucky red gem, and buried the extra jewelry in the sand.

They walked along the shore until they came to some tide pools. Pearl found a white puka shell in one of the pools. Pearl said, "If you help me find puka shells, I will help you make necklaces for your mothers."

The girls had fun collecting the shells. Before long, they had enough shells to make two necklaces. Pearl helped Janie and Karla make two beautiful necklaces from the puka shells. The girls knew that their mothers would love the necklaces.

Janie and Karla were hungry. They asked Pearl what they could eat. Pearl found a coconut. She showed Janie and Karla how to poke a hole in the coconut with a rock so that they could drink the milk. After they drank the milk, Pearl split the coconut open. Pearl gave the girls the coconut meat to eat. Janie and Karla thought it tasted delicious.

About an hour before sunset, they met Tommy at the shoreline. Janie and Karla said goodbye to Pearl and thanked Tommy and Pearl for the perfect day.

Tommy brought the girls back to where he picked them up earlier in the day. Janie and Karla gave the sea turtle hugs and kisses. They were very happy that Tommy brought them to the magical island.

When their mothers picked Janie and Karla up, the girls gave them the puka shell necklaces. Their mothers loved them.

Part 3: Stories 33–48 (2–3 pages each)

1. A _____ waved to the girls on their way to the island.
   (A) crab
   (B) dolphin
   (C) lobster
   (D) sea lion
   (E) starfish

2. The mermaid made necklaces out of _____.
   (A) diamonds
   (B) pearls
   (C) puka shells
   (D) red gems
   (E) seaweed

3. In the story, what did the girls eat?
   (A) coconut
   (B) crab
   (C) fish
   (D) lobster
   (E) seaweed

4. When did Tommy bring the girls home?
   (A) an hour after sunrise
   (B) an hour before sunset
   (C) noon
   (D) sunrise
   (E) sunset

Story #35

Royal Ball—Part 1

The girls in our class entered a contest. The winning class would be invited to attend a royal party at the king's palace. It was an essay contest. We needed to write an essay about what it takes to be a princess.

Our teacher is Miss Sandra. She is the one who encouraged us to enter the contest. Miss Sandra told us that we are all princesses. She asked us to think about how and why we are princesses, and to put this in writing.

Miss Sandra suggested that we think of each girl in our class and how she is a princess. We would use that to prepare an example of what it takes to be a princess. We would combine our ideas into an essay.

Cindy shows that it takes kindness to be a princess. Cindy is very caring. One day when Cindy was walking home from school, she saw a kindergarten girl crying. The kindergartner's name was Kelly. Cindy stopped and asked Kelly what was wrong. Kelly kept crying. Cindy stayed with her and calmed her down. It took a while, but Kelly finally opened up and explained why she had been crying. Cindy helped Kelly feel better. Kelly was amazed that an older girl cared so much about a little kindergarten girl. That's just one of many ways that Cindy demonstrates kindness.

When we thought about Stacy, we realized that a princess must show compassion. Stacy always helps those who are less fortunate. She donates her time and even part of her allowance to help others. Stacy does volunteer work after school.

Part 3: Stories 33–48 (2–3 pages each)

A princess should also show courage. Beverly is a good example of this. Beverly isn't afraid to stand up and defend herself. She also stands up for her friends. Just the other day, Beverly saw Mary being bullied by two other students. Beverly came over, supported Mary, and helped all three resolve their differences.

Sally is very beautiful. We realized that a princess should have beauty—not necessarily physical beauty, but beauty within. Although Sally is beautiful on the outside, she has inner beauty, too. It's her inner beauty that makes the biggest impression. Sally does many nice things for other people. She does small things, like lending a hand to help carry a heavy bag, but she also helps in big ways, like showing positive leadership and serving as a good role model for others.

When we thought about Patti, we decided that a princess should care about animals as well as people. Patti loves animals. If she finds a wounded animal, Patti nurses it until it heals or brings it to a veterinarian. The animals seem to sense that she loves them because stray cats, dogs, and other animals often come to her house. Patti would have a hundred pets if she could, but her parents only let her have one horse, two dogs, two cats, five parakeets, and one hamster. Patti takes care of strays just long enough so that she can find them new homes.

With motivation from Miss Sandra, the girls finished writing the essay. Miss Sandra took it to the post office and mailed it to the palace.

Guess what. One month later, Miss Sandra received a letter from the king. Miss Sandra read the letter that the king sent to our class:

Dear Students of Miss Sandra's Class,

It was my honor to read all the essays that were entered into the contest. As there were many excellent essays, choosing just one winner proved to be a difficult task.

After careful consideration, we selected your class as the winner. Every girl in your class has demonstrated that she is indeed a true princess. Therefore, it is my pleasure to invite your class to attend a royal party at our palace.

The queen's seamstress will be contacting you soon. She will fit each girl for a special gown. Each girl will be able to pick out the fabric and color for her gown. Everyone will also be fitted for matching shoes.

Miss Sandra, you must be very proud of your students. You will also be fitted for shoes and a gown.

On the day of the royal party, a carriage will be waiting at your school to bring you to the palace. It is a golden carriage pulled by six white horses.

The queen and I look forward to meeting each of you. The royal dinner and dance will be held in your honor.

      Sincerely,

      King & Queen Thames

Part 3: Stories 33–48 (2–3 pages each)

1. Cindy demonstrated kindness by _____.
    (A) doing volunteer work after school
    (B) helping a kindergartner
    (C) helping wounded animals
    (D) lending a hand to help carry a heavy bag
    (E) supporting a student who was being bullied

2. Stacy demonstrated compassion by _____.
    (A) doing volunteer work after school
    (B) helping a kindergartner
    (C) helping wounded animals
    (D) lending a hand to help carry a heavy bag
    (E) supporting a student who was being bullied

3. The class determined that a princess should have inner beauty.
    (A) true
    (B) false

4. Miss Sandra's class won the contest.
    (A) true
    (B) false

Story #36

Royal Ball—Part 2

The girls in Miss Sandra's class won a contest to attend a royal party at the king's palace. The girls were very excited the day when the queen's seamstress came to fit them for their special gowns and shoes.

This was the first time that any of the girls had a custom dress made for them. Eloise, the seamstress, explained the dress-making process.

Eloise took the measurements of each girl. She said that this was the first step of making the perfect gown.

Next, each girl chose the style she wanted for her gown. The girls browsed through a catalog showing sample gowns. Eloise asked each girl a few questions to help her choose a pattern. "What type of neckline do you like? Do you prefer to have sleeves? Which of these styles do you like?"

Once each girl selected a style, she picked the fabric and color. Eloise helped the girls choose their colors, suggesting how hair and eye color might coordinate with the gown.

Sally selected a long, flowing gown with a train. The light green satin fabric Sally chose matched her green eyes. Eloise suggested sewing rhinestones around the neckline. Sally thought that would be beautiful.

Cindy couldn't decide what style dress would be best for her. All she knew was that she wanted a pink chiffon gown. Eloise told her that an A-line gown is better suited for chiffon fabric. Cindy agreed to try that.

Part 3: Stories 33–48 (2–3 pages each)

Beverly knew exactly what she wanted. She picked a sleeveless gown so that she could wear matching long gloves. Beverly wanted her gown to be made with light yellow satin and gold lace. Her gown would include ruffles along the hemline.

Patti selected a fabric with leopard print because she loves animals. Eloise suggested a simple fitted gown.

Stacy dreams of being a fashion designer. She gave plenty of thought to selecting her design. Stacy chose a turquoise silk gown. She asked Eloise if she could sew hundreds of pearls on it. "Of course I can," replied Eloise. "Would you like matching earrings and a necklace, too?" Stacy gladly accepted her offer.

Four weeks after the fitting, Eloise returned to their school. Eloise brought the gowns and shoes with her, along with her assistants. The girls tried on their gowns. Eloise and her assistants made adjustments, as needed.

The girls also tried on their shoes. Most of the girls chose a low heel, but Sally wanted flats because she is already tall to begin with. Each girl's shoes matched her gown.

Everyone looked stunning. They were busy checking their reflections in the mirrors, and seeing how their classmates looked. Every girl gave and received many compliments.

Eloise surprised the girls with tiaras. She told them that every princess must wear a tiara. The tiaras were made of jewels that matched the colors of their gowns.

Before she left, Eloise asked each girl which accessories she would like. She knew that Beverly wanted matching gloves and that Stacy wanted pearl earrings and necklace. Did anyone else want gloves, jewelry, or a handbag?

Eloise informed them that she would have their gowns and accessories ready the week before the big event.

On the morning of the party, the girls were taken to a beauty salon. The stylist cut, trimmed, and styled their hair. Patti wanted her long hair in a French braid. Cindy liked hers pinned up with a few curls hanging loose around her face. Beverly has naturally curly hair. The stylist thought that Beverly would look cute showing off her long, natural curls. Sally decided to have flowers braided in her long blond hair. Stacy liked that idea, too, and asked to have flowers braided in her black hair.

Miss Sandra always wore her hair in a tight bun. The girls convinced Miss Sandra to wear her hair down. When the stylist finished her hairdo, the girls were amazed at how beautiful Miss Sandra's hair was. They told her that she should always wear her hair hanging loosely around her pretty face.

After the girls had their hair styled, they were brought back to school to finish getting dressed. Eloise helped the girls put their gowns on without messing up their hair. She also helped them with their accessories and tiaras.

All of the princesses looked beautiful in their gowns. Their gowns matched how beautiful they were on the inside.

Everyone was very excited. They could hardly stand still waiting for the carriage to arrive. They knew it was going to be the best day of their lives (so far).

Part 3: Stories 33–48 (2–3 pages each)

1. Who is the seamstress?
   - (A) Beverly
   - (B) Cindy
   - (C) Eloise
   - (D) Patti
   - (E) Sally

2. When would the gowns be ready?
   - (A) immediately
   - (B) on the day of the party
   - (C) one day before the party
   - (D) one month before the party
   - (E) one week before the party

3. The seamstress surprised the girls with _____.
   - (A) gloves
   - (B) gowns
   - (C) necklaces
   - (D) shoes
   - (E) tiaras

4. The students like it best when Miss Sandra _____.
   - (A) braids her hair
   - (B) curls her hair
   - (C) decorates her hair with flowers
   - (D) lets her hair hang loosely
   - (E) wears her hair in a bun

Story #37

Royal Ball—Part 3

Miss Sandra and the princesses were waiting for the carriage to arrive, which would bring them to the party at the palace. They looked splendid in their custom-made gowns, matching shoes, and tiaras with sparkling gems.

Cindy was the first to spot the carriage. "Look, look! Here comes the golden carriage. It is being pulled by six white horses."

The chauffeur greeted everyone, and then helped Miss Sandra and the princesses into the carriage. The inside of the carriage was as elegant as the outside. The seats were plush red velvet, which they sank into when they sat down. It was a very exciting ride to the palace.

As they approached the palace, they saw golden gates that opened to the palace grounds. There were thousands of colorful flowers and the bushes were trimmed in the shapes of many different animals. A path through the gardens led to the palace.

When the princesses saw the palace they were awestruck. It was larger and more ornate than they had imagined. It also featured golden trim that matched the carriage and gates. The girls looked up and saw the king and queen waving to them from the balcony. They waved back and smiled.

The chauffeur parked the carriage in front of the entry doors to the palace. He helped the girls out of the carriage and led them to a red carpet leading to the palace. The guards saluted them as they walked past.

Part 3: Stories 33–48 (2–3 pages each)

Everyone was greeted by the captain of the king's guard as they entered the parlor. The captain presented each girl with a wrist corsage. Each corsage was specially made for each girl: The flowers matched their gowns.

The girls were led to the reception room. The king and queen were waiting there. The king and queen greeted the girls as they entered. Miss Sandra and the princesses politely curtsied as they met the king and queen. They had a very long, polite conversation with the king and queen. Because the king was so impressed with the girls, he told them that they truly were princesses.

When it was time to eat, the girls followed the king and queen into the formal dining room. The dining room was huge. The dining table was surprisingly long and was set with elegant china and silverware. The walls were mirrored, which made the room look like it went on forever.

The king reminded Miss Sandra and the princesses that this dinner was held in their honor. The food was delicious. They were served a seven-course dinner. It started with caviar for the appetizer. Roast duckling with applesauce was the main entrée. For dessert, they ate chocolate and vanilla cream puffs.

The waiters stayed close by and frequently checked that everything was excellent. The waiters refilled their glasses with their favorite drinks before the glass was half empty. They offered second servings on everything.

There was just one problem with the dinner: The girls were puzzled about which forks and spoons to use. Fortunately, the waiters politely whispered words of advice to help the girls use the proper utensils.

After dinner, the girls were led to the ballroom. The dance floor was bigger than their school gym. The king and queen led the first dance. After the king danced with the queen, he danced with Miss Sandra. When the king finished dancing with Miss Sandra, the king and queen each danced with all of the princesses.

The girls felt honored to dance with the king and queen. They could hardly believe that it was really happening to them. Sally pinched herself, but didn't wake up. It was real!

After the dance, the captain of the king's guard took the girls on a tour of the palace. They climbed a long winding staircase that led to a turret. Turrets are small towers on top of the palace. In the olden days, the guards would be stationed in the turrets when danger was present. Now the turrets are no longer needed for defensive purposes. From there, the girls could see for miles. The captain pointed out the moat that still surrounds the palace. It is a deep ditch filled with water. In the original design, it offered a layer of protection to the palace.

They walked back down the staircase, and then went outside to see the drawbridge. The captain explained how in the olden days the drawbridge would be raised when there was danger. Although the drawbridge is no longer used, the captain raised it so that the girls could see how it worked.

The room that impressed the girls the most was the throne room. Three steps led up to the throne. The throne was gold-plated, and had red and gold satin cushions. The royal crowns were stored in a glass case beside the throne. The diamonds and gems were sparkling.

Patti said, "Imagine sitting on the throne wearing the queen's crown. That would be awesome!" The other girls agreed with her.

When it was time to leave, Miss Sandra and the princesses said their goodbyes and thanked the king and queen for the wonderful day. It was a day fit for a princess.

Part 3: Stories 33–48 (2–3 pages each)

1. The bushes were shaped like _____.
    (A) animals
    (B) jewels
    (C) princes and princesses
    (D) royal crowns
    (E) the king and queen

2. The turrets are still needed for defensive purposes.
    (A) true
    (B) false

3. Who gave the girls a tour of the palace?
    (A) Miss Sandra
    (B) the captain of the guards
    (C) the king
    (D) the queen
    (E) the seamstress

4. During the tour, the _____ impressed the girls most.
    (A) drawbridge
    (B) moat
    (C) staircase
    (D) throne room
    (E) turret

Story #38

Slumber Mystery

Carla planned an ordinary slumber party, but it didn't turn out that way. Like many sleepovers, there was pizza and they told stories at bedtime. However, unlike most slumber parties, Carla's party had a mystery to solve.

After all of Carla's friends arrived and put their sleeping bags and pajamas aside, Carla told them about the mystery.

Carla explained that she had a pink teddy bear wearing a blue sweater with a red heart. This teddy bear, named Cupcake, was supposed to be the slumber party mascot. Unfortunately, Cupcake disappeared before the party ever started.

Carla's friends wanted to help her solve the mystery. Carla offered a reward: The winner would choose the first party game.

The girls needed to think like detectives and search the house for clues. Several questions came to mind. Did someone take Cupcake, or was he lost? Who would take him? Suspects included Carla's little sister, Cassidy, her older brother, Jack, and even her parents. They didn't really think that Carla's parents would hide her party mascot, but all clues had to be followed.

Tracy ran to Jack's bedroom. Tracy knew that Jack had teased Carla and her friends in the past. Tracy looked under Jack's bed, in his closet, and even checked behind his computer desk. She didn't see any sign of Cupcake.

Becky was sure that she would find Cupcake in Cassidy's bedroom. The last time Becky had been to Carla's house, there had been many stuffed animals in Cassidy's room. Becky

Part 3: Stories 33–48 (2–3 pages each)

suspected that Cassidy wanted to have Cupcake, too. Becky looked through Cassidy's stuffed animal collection, which she had on her bed and bookshelves. Cupcake wasn't there, nor was he in Cassidy's closet.

Betsy decided to check Carla's parents' bedroom. It didn't take long to check because their bedroom was tidy. Betsy looked under the bed and in the closet, just in case. She also checked behind the drapes, but didn't find Cupcake.

Diana and Kathy checked all of the bathrooms. They looked behind the toilets, in the bathtub, and behind the shower curtains. Kathy also checked the linen closet. Cupcake wasn't in any of those places.

So far, no one had found Cupcake. Where could he be?

Annie looked through everything in the kitchen. Cupcake wasn't in any of the cabinets, on the counter, or in the refrigerator. Annie was about to leave the kitchen when she noticed the doggie door. Annie had an idea. Maybe Carla's puppy, named Snoopy, took Cupcake. Annie opened the back door and went to Snoopy's doghouse. Cupcake was snuggled up next to Snoopy. Annie didn't want to take Cupcake from Snoopy, so she ran inside to get Carla.

Carla and the other girls followed Annie outside to Snoopy's doghouse. Carla giggled when she looked inside Snoopy's doghouse. Carla gently pried Cupcake from Snoopy.

All the girls hugged Annie and congratulated her. They told her that she was a great detective.

As Annie's reward, she got to choose the first party game. She thought it would be a good idea to play the first game with Snoopy. They had Snoopy to thank for making the slumber party interesting with a mystery. Everyone agreed. They went outside and played Frisbee with Snoopy.

1. Whose slumber party was it?
    (A) Annie's
    (B) Becky's
    (C) Betsy's
    (D) Carla's
    (E) Diana's

2. What reward was offered for finding Cupcake?
    (A) choose the first party game
    (B) free Frisbee
    (C) get to keep Cupcake
    (D) movie passes
    (E) one slice of pizza

3. _____ found Cupcake.
    (A) Annie
    (B) Becky
    (C) Betsy
    (D) Carla
    (E) Diana

4. Cupcake was found in _____.
    (A) Carla's parents' bedroom
    (B) Cassidy's bedroom
    (C) Jack's bedroom
    (D) the doghouse
    (E) the kitchen

Part 3: Stories 33–48 (2–3 pages each)

Story #39

County Fair

Morgan, Taylor, and Maria are best friends. They have been friends ever since they were two or three years old. They do nearly everything together. So when Taylor's mother told her that they were going to the county fair, she naturally asked if Morgan and Maria could come along with her. They were all quite happy when her mother agreed.

Morgan and Maria slept over at Taylor's house the night before the big day. They stayed up late talking about all the fun things they wanted to do at the fair. It seemed that they were laughing and giggling most of the night. They had trouble sleeping because they were very excited. When they finally did sleep, they even dreamed about the fair.

When Taylor's mother came in to wake the girls, she was surprised to see them already dressed and ready to go. Taylor's mother said, "Wow! You girls must be really excited to visit the fair. Hmm. Why aren't you up and ready before the alarm goes off on school mornings?"

The girls giggled and told Taylor's mother that they couldn't wait to get the day started.

As soon as they went through the fair entrance, the girls knew where they wanted to go. They ran straight to the roller coaster. They wanted to go on the fastest, scariest ride first. Morgan and Maria sat in the front row, while Taylor and her mother sat in the second row. It sure was fun, but they wouldn't admit that they were a little scared.

When they walked by the dunk tank, the girls begged Taylor's mother to get on the platform above the water so that they could try to dunk her. Taylor's mother laughed, but agreed to it because she didn't think they could dunk her. Each girl had one turn to throw the baseball at the target. There were no second chances.

Taylor had the first chance to dunk her mother. She threw the baseball as hard as she could, but didn't come close to the target.

Morgan took the next turn at throwing the baseball. She wound up carefully. When she threw the ball, it looked like a great shot. Taylor and Maria screamed because she was so close—but not close enough.

Now it was Maria's turn. Morgan's mother didn't know that Maria was a great softball pitcher. Morgan and Taylor cheered Maria on. "Go Maria. Keep your eye on the target. We know you can do it!"

Taylor's mother laughed and said, "Just throw the ball so we can get something to eat."

Maria stayed focused, and was determined to hit the target. She silently counted to three and then threw the ball. She hit the target. The force of the impact released the lever that was holding Taylor's mother on the platform. Taylor's mother fell in with a big splash. A crowd quickly appeared to see what had happened.

The girls picked up a towel and handed it to Taylor's mother. As she was drying off, Taylor's mother asked, "Where did you get that arm?"

Maria told her how she had been playing softball with her brothers since she was very little. They taught her how to pitch. Now she's the pitcher on her softball team.

Part 3: Stories 33–48 (2–3 pages each)

Taylor's mother was a good sport. She told Maria that she was very impressed. She said it actually felt good to get wet because it was a hot day.

She added, "Okay. Now it's time to get something to eat. What would you girls like? You might want to pick something that you don't normally get to eat. It will be my treat."

Taylor loves cheese so she decided to try the mac and cheese with bacon bits. Morgan thought a double bacon corn dog sounded good. Maria dared to try something new called a hot beef sundae. It is beef with gravy, corn, and cheese topped with a cherry tomato. It is served in a bowl to make it look like a sundae. Taylor's mother wasn't quite as daring as the girls. She had chicken on a stick with fried cheese.

They enjoyed their meals and had fun sampling each other's foods. After filling their tummies they headed to the arcade. They thought it would be a good idea to let their lunch digest before they went on any fast rides.

At the arcade, Morgan won a big white bear holding a red heart. She had fun carrying it around the rest of the day. They went on every ride twice.

The girls had so much fun, they couldn't thank Taylor's mother enough. Taylor's mother gave them something to look forward to by telling them that she would take them again next year.

1. What did they do first at the fair?
    (A) ate snacks
    (B) played arcade games
    (C) rode a Ferris Wheel
    (D) threw baseballs at a target
    (E) went on a roller coaster

2. Taylor's mother yelled at the girls for getting her wet.
    (A) true
    (B) false

3. Morgan won a _____.
    (A) bear
    (B) cat
    (C) dog
    (D) frog
    (E) lion

4. Taylor's mother offered to take the girls again next year.
    (A) true
    (B) false

Part 3: Stories 33–48 (2–3 pages each)

Story #40

Mermaid Surprise—Part 1

Savannah's family has a beach house. Every year, they visit the beach house during their summer vacation. For as long as she can remember, Savannah has loved mermaids. Every time she swims in the ocean, she looks for a mermaid. Savannah is sure that one day she will see one. When she is not swimming in search of mermaids, she is reading about them.

One time, Savannah overheard her mother, Jeannine, tell a friend, "All Savannah thinks about are mermaids. She probably dreams about them, too!" Savannah didn't say anything, but she thought to herself, "It's true!"

This was also true on the morning of her birthday. Savannah had been dreaming about meeting a mermaid. When she woke up, she had no idea what her parents had planned for her birthday.

When Savannah walked into the kitchen, she found her father, Frank, drinking a cup of coffee. He wished her a happy birthday, and said that he would take her to breakfast for her birthday.

While they were out of the house, her mother began to decorate for a surprise mermaid birthday. Jeannine hung under-the-sea decorations, like pictures of starfish and sea plants, throughout the house. Balloons were shaped like fish, crabs, and whales. Driftwood and seashells decorated the table. The centerpiece was a large cake in the shape of a mermaid.

The first thing Savannah saw when they pulled in the driveway was a huge banner hanging on the garage. It read: "Happy Birthday, Savannah the Mermaid Princess!"

It was really quiet when Savannah and her father walked into the house. Savannah wondered where her mother was. As Savannah walked into the family room, her mother and all of her friends started singing a song to wish her a happy birthday.

Savannah's mother and friends all rushed over and gave her big hugs. Savannah looked around and saw all the decorations. It was a fantastic birthday party. All she could say was, "Wow! Thank you so much!"

Jeannine told everyone that the party was moving outside to the beach. Jeannine had another surprise for Savannah and the party girls.

When the girls went outside, they found Savannah's mother standing beside a very large box. The girls were curious about what was inside. Jeannine asked the birthday girl to open the box.

Savannah found matching mermaid tails and tops inside the box. Each set was a different color. Jeannine said to Savannah, "It's your birthday, so you get the first pick. Which color do you want to wear?"

Savannah looked at all of them before picking the rainbow-colored mermaid outfit. Rachel picked blue, Diane picked pink, Laurie picked orange, Jenny picked green, Zoe picked yellow, Susie picked a polka-dotted outfit, and Terri picked a striped outfit. Every mermaid tail and top looked pretty.

After all the party girls selected their mermaid tails and tops, they took turns putting them on in the dressing room. Once they were all dressed and ready to go, they raced over to the shoreline.

The first party activity was to see who could collect the most seashells in five minutes. When the time was up, the girls counted

Part 3: Stories 33–48 (2–3 pages each)

how many shells they found. Savannah's friend, Rachel, found twenty-four. That was five more than anyone else had collected. Rachel won a pack of mermaid stickers.

The next activity was swimming in the ocean. Before diving in the water, Savannah yelled, "Keep an eye out for a real mermaid!"

Savannah's mother and father stood on the shore watching the eight little mermaids swimming along the shoreline. Jeannine commented, "They are having so much fun. Don't they look beautiful swimming and riding the waves? I hope Savannah finds her mermaid."

Frank replied, "Hey, do you see what I see? A real mermaid is swimming with the party girls. I think Savannah's dream just came true. She is about to have the best birthday ever!"

They watched the girls swim until the real mermaid waved goodbye to them and swam away.

The girls came out of the water laughing and giggling. Savannah yelled, "Mom and dad, did you see the real mermaid? She swam with us!"

"Yes, honey. We saw the whole thing. We took pictures, too." The girls enjoyed looking at the pictures.

Each girl received a tote bag with mermaid goodies.

The party returned back to the house. They played a couple of games before it was time for cake and ice-cream. The mermaid cake was so pretty that Savannah wished she could keep it forever, but she knew that she couldn't.

Savannah thanked everyone for making her birthday special.

1. Frank is Savannah's _____.
   (A) brother
   (B) cousin
   (C) father
   (D) friend
   (E) grandfather

2. Savannah's mother's name is _____.
   (A) Jeannine
   (B) Jenny
   (C) Rachel
   (D) Susie
   (E) Zoe

3. Savannah picked the _____ mermaid tail and top.
   (A) blue
   (B) pink
   (C) polka-dotted
   (D) rainbow-colored
   (E) striped

4. Who found the most seashells?
   (A) Jenny
   (B) Rachel
   (C) Savannah
   (D) Susie
   (E) Zoe

Part 3: Stories 33–48 (2–3 pages each)

Story #41

Mermaid Surprise—Part 2

Savannah thinks she is the luckiest girl in the world. She spends every summer at her family's beach house. She loves swimming in the ocean while looking for a mermaid.

This year, she had the best birthday any girl could have. Her mom threw a surprise mermaid birthday party for her. Seven of Savannah's best friends helped her celebrate her special day. Her mom gave the girls mermaid tails and matching tops so that they could swim in the ocean like mermaids.

Savannah's wish to see a mermaid came true on her birthday. She had always looked for a real mermaid every time she swam in the ocean. While the eight party mermaids were swimming, a real mermaid came up to them and swam with them.

Since her birthday, Savannah has been swimming in the ocean every day looking for the mermaid. She keeps looking, but hasn't seen her again.

Today, Savannah was swimming with her friend, Rachel. They were swimming like mermaids, wearing their mermaid tails and matching tops. They were hoping to be lucky again and swim with the real mermaid. They wished they had asked the mermaid what her name was and where to find her. Unfortunately, they don't know anything about the mermaid, except what she looks like and that she is a really good swimmer.

Rachel suggested that they go to the lagoon. It sounded like fun to Savannah so they gave it a try. The lagoon is always beautiful. While swimming like mermaids, they enjoyed looking at all the beautifully colored fish. They also saw several starfish.

After a while, they decided to climb up on the rocky bluffs to rest and soak in the warm sunshine. Savannah looked up and saw her mother, Jeannine, walking towards them. Jeannine was carrying a picnic basket. As Jeannine neared them, she said, "Hi, girls. I thought you would be hungry."

Jeannine found a sandy spot on which to spread out a blanket and set up their lunch. The girls didn't realize how hungry and thirsty they were until they started eating. Savannah and Rachel enjoyed looking down at the lagoon while eating their lunch.

After lunch, the girls built a sand castle. They mixed the sand and water to form the towers. Then they carved staircases into the towers. They built walls to connect the towers. They cut tunnels in the walls. The sand castle grew larger and larger. The main tower was almost three feet tall. Afterward, they formed a mermaid in the sand.

The girls were so busy carving the mermaid in the sand that they didn't hear anything else around them. It startled them when they heard someone comment, "That's an amazing sand castle!"

When the girls looked up, they saw the mermaid that swam with them on Savannah's birthday. Savannah said, "Thanks! We have been looking for you every day. What is your name?"

"My name is Muriel. My parents named me after the shining sea. What are your names?"

Part 3: Stories 33–48 (2–3 pages each)

The girls introduced themselves. Savannah said, "I want to know all about you. Where do you sleep? Do you have friends? Please, tell us everything about yourself."

"I live in an underwater cave with my sisters. I have many sea friends. My sisters and friends are shy around people. They like staying together. They aren't as adventurous as I am."

Rachel asked, "What do you eat?"

"I eat sea food. My favorites are shrimp, lobster, and crab. Would you like to swim with me?" Of course they would!

They all dove into the ocean. They swam in and out of the waves. Muriel pointed to something in the distance. When they got closer, they saw that it was a school of dolphins. The dolphins looked beautiful riding the waves and playing together. It was incredible. The dolphins made bubble rings with their blowholes. Some of them would spin the bubbles with their beaks, and others broke them apart by biting them. It was really fun to watch.

Savannah and Rachel followed Muriel as she swam back towards the lagoon. When they reached the lagoon, Muriel swam around for a while. It seemed like she was looking for something. Soon they saw her pick up something. Muriel motioned for the girls to get out of the water with her. When they returned to their sand castle, they discovered what Muriel had just picked up. Muriel gave them each a sand dollar to remember her by. Muriel said that she had to go, but promised that she would see them again another day.

1. What does the name Muriel mean?
    (A) from the shore
    (B) sand castle
    (C) sand dollar
    (D) sea and sky
    (E) shining sea

2. Muriel sleeps _____.
    (A) in a hidden city
    (B) in a large clam shell
    (C) in an underwater cave
    (D) on the bluff
    (E) on the rocks

3. Muriel gave each girl _____.
    (A) a dolphin
    (B) a sand castle
    (C) a sand dollar
    (D) a sandwich
    (E) seaweed

4. According to the story, all mermaids are very adventurous.
    (A) true
    (B) false

Story #42

Mermaid Surprise—Part 3

Savannah and Rachel were swimming in the lagoon near Savannah's family beach house. They were hoping to once again see a mermaid named Muriel.

The girls first met Muriel on Savannah's birthday. When the party girls dressed up with mermaid fins and tops and swam in the ocean, Muriel had shown up to swim alongside them. The second time Savannah and Rachel saw Muriel was when they had built a sand castle near the lagoon. They were hoping to see Muriel a third time today.

The girls were wearing their mermaid fins and matching tops. They wished that they could swim like Muriel. When Muriel swims, it looks like she is gliding effortlessly through the water. Rachel was hoping that Muriel will give them some tips on how to swim better. Savannah and Rachel wondered why they hadn't seen Muriel lately. The last time they saw her, Muriel promised that she would see them again.

Savannah and Rachel practiced swimming like mermaids until their muscles were sore. The girls decided to rest for a while. They found a nice sandy place by the lagoon where they could kick back and relax.

Once the girls recovered, they felt bored and went exploring. They spotted a couple of sand crabs. Savannah and Rachel thought it would be fun to have a crab race.

Savannah named one Mr. Crab. Rachel named the other Hermie (short for hermit crab).

On your marks… Get set… Go! The girls released the crabs from their starting positions. The crabs began crawling—sideways, of course. Hermie was crawling toward the finish line. Mr. Crab took off really fast, but was heading the wrong way.

Savannah cried, "Oh no, Mr. Crab. You'll lose the race if you go that way. Please turn around."

While Savannah tried to persuade Mr. Crab to turn around, Hermie crossed the finish line.

The girls turned around when they heard someone say, "Hi, Savannah! Hi, Rachel!"

It was the mermaid, Muriel. The girls hugged Muriel and told her how happy they were to see her.

Rachel said, "We were talking about you this morning, Muriel. We would like you to help us learn to swim gracefully like you do."

Muriel told Savannah and Rachel that she would love to help them learn to swim better. Muriel asked the girls to stand on the shore and watch her swim for a while. Muriel said to pay close attention to how she does her dolphin kick. When the dolphin kick is done right, it sends a ripple along the swimmer's body.

Savannah and Rachel watched Muriel swim until she motioned for the girls to join her. Muriel said, "Now it's your turn to swim."

The girls practiced their dolphin kicks. Muriel was impressed. "You have both improved very much. I think you are ready for an adventure. Would you like to see where I live and meet my sisters?" Of course they would!

Muriel brought Savannah and Rachel to an underwater cave where Muriel lives with her sisters. Muriel's sisters are shy. It took them a while to warm up to Savannah and Rachel. Once the mermaids felt comfortable with the girls, they had fun showing them their home.

Part 3: Stories 33–48 (2–3 pages each)

Their cave was beautiful. It was in a coral reef where starfish decorated the ocean floor. Butterfly fish swam throughout their living room. The mermaids had seaweed beds. Three giant manta rays lived outside of the mermaids' home. The manta rays were friends with the mermaids.

Muriel asked if Savannah and Rachel wanted to go for a ride. The girls rode on the back of a manta ray named Manny. Muriel and her sisters swam alongside them. The manta ray was a graceful swimmer like Muriel.

Manny told the girls to hold on. He showed them how acrobatic he is. They held on tight while he leapt in and out of the water. To Savannah and Rachel, riding on Manny's back was more exciting than any roller coaster.

Muriel suggested that they explore a sunken ship that was near the mermaids' cave. Muriel's sister, Rivera, found the sunken ship years ago. Rivera loves sparkly things. One day when Rivera was swimming, she saw something shiny. When she went in for a closer look, Rivera saw the wrecked ship. The shiny object was a mirrored chest.

Savannah, Rachel, Manny, and the mermaids went to the sunken ship. They had fun exploring the sunken ship together. Rivera showed them where she had found her treasure. Rachel spotted something shiny. Rachel pointed at it. Rivera dove down for a closer look. When Rivera returned, she had something in her hand. It was a golden nugget. She offered it to Rachel.

It was getting late, so the girls needed to head back home. Manny gave the girls a ride to the shore while Muriel and Rivera swam along. They all said goodbye and promised to see each other again. Savannah and Rachel thanked the mermaids and Manny for the super fun day.

1. Manny is _____.
    (A) a manta ray
    (B) a mermaid
    (C) Rachel's brother
    (D) Savannah's brother
    (E) Savannah's father

2. Rivera is _____.
    (A) a manta ray
    (B) Muriel's sister
    (C) Muriel's mother
    (D) Rachel's sister
    (E) Savannah's sister

3. Which crab won the crab race?
    (A) Hermie
    (B) Mr. Crab
    (C) neither—it was a tie.

4. Savannah and Rachel swam better after they perfected the _____.
    (A) backstroke
    (B) breathing exercises
    (C) dolphin kick
    (D) floating technique
    (E) leg extension

Story #43

Martian Guide

It started out like any other school morning in Anchorage, Alaska. Destiny was at the school bus stop waiting for the bus to arrive when she heard a whirling noise. She looked up in the sky and saw a spaceship hovering above. She wondered what was happening.

A little green man opened the door and said, "Please, come aboard my spaceship."

Destiny was about to turn around and run as fast as she could, until she saw Charlie, her bus driver. Destiny was still confused about what was going on.

When Destiny looked into the spaceship, she noticed that Charlie was sitting in the seat next to the alien. Destiny looked at Charlie and asked, "Where is the school bus?"

Charlie answered, "Marty is a Martian. He will bring you to school today in his spaceship."

Destiny climbed aboard and took the seat next to Charlie.

Marty asked, "Would you like to take the scenic route on the way to your school today?"

"Sure," replied Destiny. "It sounds like fun. Let's go."

"My spaceship can travel as fast as light. Don't worry though: We won't go that fast. We will go just fast enough so that we can travel around the world before you have to be at school. You will get to see the earth, and we will fly low enough for you to enjoy the scenery. As we go, I will show you some points of interest."

Destiny was excited. "I can't wait."

"We are already flying over Canada. If you look below, you will see Banff National Park in Alberta. Look at the beautiful mountains. I've heard people say that it is a popular vacation spot for skiers."

Marty handed Destiny a special pair of glasses so that she could get a close-up view of the landscape.

"Next we will fly over the Mount Rushmore National Memorial in South Dakota. If you wear your special glasses, you can see the four United States presidents carved in stone. The head sculptures of Thomas Jefferson, George Washington, Teddy Roosevelt, and Abe Lincoln are each about sixty feet tall."

Destiny asked, "Marty, how do you know so much. Did you learn all of this at school on Mars?"

Marty started laughing. "That's silly! We don't have schools on Mars. I travel all over in my spaceship. I study everything I see. Sometimes I stop and pick up earth people. I learn a great deal by having conversations with them."

"I was about to run away from your spaceship, until I recognized Charlie. How do you get other people to talk to you or take a ride? Aren't they scared when they see your spaceship?"

"Many earthlings are interested in outer space, especially Mars. I can always find people who are more curious than afraid. Some people have offered to pay me to take them out into space, but I don't accept money."

Destiny wondered, "Why don't you take their money?"

"I have no use for money," replied Marty. "You earth people are the only ones who value money and material things. We live a simple life on Mars."

"Wow. Life without money would sure be strange."

"Look over there." Marty pointed. "It's the Statue of Liberty. She is over one hundred feet tall."

Destiny looked through her special glasses. "That's amazing!"

"Now we will fly down the East coast of the United States and then over Mexico." A short while later, Marty announced. "Now you can see Cancun, Mexico. See how clear the ocean water is."

Minutes later, Marty said, "We are now flying over Brazil. If you look quickly, you will see Sugarloaf Mountain in Rio de Janeiro. I bet you would love the annual carnival in Rio de Janeiro. I heard that it is the carnival capital of the world."

After a while, Charlie pointed and asked, "Look! Look! Are those the pyramids in Egypt?"

"Good eye, Charlie. Yes, they are. Aren't they incredible?"

"Yes, they are," both Charlie and Destiny answered.

"We are running out of time," said Marty. "We need to speed this up. I will show you Big Ben in London, the Swiss Alps, the Great Wall of China, and the Kremlin in Moscow. Then we'll need to get back to Anchorage so you'll get to school on time."

"Your spaceship really is fast," said Destiny, "if we're able to see so many places and not be late for school."

Marty said, "I wish we had more time. Maybe you can take a field trip with me one day. I could slow this spaceship down a bit and show you every country and landmark."

Charlie and Destiny both answered at the same time. "Yes! That would be fantastic!"

"Well, we are back in Alaska. There is your school." Marty pointed. "I will drop you off now."

"Thank you! That was a trip of a lifetime," said Destiny.

Everyone shook hands and said their goodbyes.

1. Destiny lives _____.
    (A) in Alaska
    (B) in Canada
    (C) in Mexico
    (D) in South Dakota
    (E) on Mars

2. Mount Rushmore features _____ carved in stone.
    (A) a carnival
    (B) a great wall
    (C) money
    (D) presidents
    (E) pyramids

3. Where is the carnival capital of the world?
    (A) Alaska
    (B) Brazil
    (C) Canada
    (D) Mexico
    (E) South Dakota

4. How much does Marty charge for a tour?
    (A) $10 per mile
    (B) nothing
    (C) the cost of gas

Part 3: Stories 33–48 (2–3 pages each)

Story #44

Fairy World

Kelli went to the greatest amusement park in the world. It's called Fairy World. It has real fairies. You won't find Fairy World on a map or in the phone book. You have to meet a real fairy in order to receive an invitation.

Kelli first heard about Fairy World from her friends. She was very excited when she met a fairy and received an invitation.

When Kelli told her friends about her invitation, they told her to go on the Land of Fairies ride first. They told Kelli that it's the best ride, but they wouldn't explain why. Kelli's friends didn't want to spoil the fun by giving away what happens. All they would tell her was, "There is no ride like it. It's better than the best dream you could ever have."

Kelli was excited just thinking about it.

When Kelli went to Fairy World, she headed straight to the Land of Fairies ride. As soon as Kelli buckled her seatbelt, the ride began. Up and away she went.

She was flying over the Land of Fairies. It wasn't a roller coaster. There wasn't a track. There weren't any cables. Her seat just traveled through the air.

Kelli looked down at hundreds of dolls. Kelli had never seen so many beautiful dolls. The gardens were filled with thousands of flowers in every color. Butterflies were fluttering among the flowers. Kelli was enjoying all the beauty.

As she was flying over the gardens, dolls were coming to life. The dolls sang and danced.

One of the fairies flew right next to Kelli. The fairy was friendly and very talkative. She asked Kelli if she would like to fly with them.

Kelli answered, "I wish I could fly, but I can't. If I step off this ride, I'll fall down."

The fairy told Kelli, "If you wish really hard, you'll be able to fly in Fairy World. You have to believe in yourself and try hard."

Kelli thought it sounded silly, but she really wanted to fly. Kelli wished as hard as she could. She thought, "Please let me fly."

Suddenly, Kelli grew wings. They were beautiful—just like the wings of the fairies, but larger. They were blue and glittery.

Kelli unbuckled her seatbelt and flapped her wings. She really could fly! Kelli flew along with the fairies. More and more of the dolls had come to life. It was fantastic!

Fairies down below were singing and dancing. Kelli flew down to see them. She sang and danced with the fairies. They sang, "It's a lovely day for a fairy in the Land of Fairies. We are happy. We are smiling. We can do anything we put our minds to. It's great to be a fairy."

Kelli flew around, exploring the rest of Fairy World. A few of the fairies flew along with her. The sweet smell of pastries told her they were getting close to the Land of the Sweets. Fairies were taking cookies, cakes, and doughnuts out of an oven.

The sweets smelled delicious. Kelli had worked up an appetite flying and dancing so she stopped to eat some sweets. Kelli first ate a chocolate-filled éclair. One of the fairies gave her a basket to fill with her choice of freshly baked sweets. Kelli picked up chocolate chip cookies, strawberry shortcake, cupcakes of every flavor, banana-cream pie, and lemon meringue pie. Her basket was filled to the brim.

Part 3: Stories 33–48 (2–3 pages each)

Kelli sat down at a picnic table next to a waterfall that flowed into a pool. Fairies were flying through the waterfall and swimming in the pool. It was a beautiful setting. Kelli ate her desserts while she watched the fairies. Kelli ate and ate, yet she didn't get full. Kelli was surprised that she was able to eat so much, without feeling full. She asked one of the fairies about this.

The fairy told Kelli that their sweets have magical properties. She could eat as many as her heart desires, but never be full.

When Kelli finished her basket of goodies, she flew to the Land of Happiness. Everyone is happy in the Land of Happiness. Everyone is nice to everyone else. It made Kelli feel very peaceful and content to be there. She smiled.

Next, Kelli flew to the Land of Rides. There were swing sets, roller coasters, bumper cars, trains, wagon rides, parachutes, water rides, and just about every kind of ride you could imagine. Kelli went on every ride twice, but none were as exciting as the Land of Fairies ride.

Her friends were right: The Land of Fairies ride was the best ride ever! Kelli wished that her world was like the Land of Happiness. She thought that it would be wonderful to live in a place where everyone is kind to one another. She could imagine how sweet it would be to see everyone smiling.

1. What happened when Kelli was riding the Land of Fairies?
    (A) Fairies sang a happy birthday song to her.
    (B) Kelli's best friend got on the ride with her.
    (C) The dolls came to life.
    (D) The ride broke down.
    (E) all of the above

2. Which of the following happened in the story?
    (A) Kelli cried when it was time to go home.
    (B) Kelli got full after eating the strawberry shortcake.
    (C) Kelli grew wings and flew in the air.
    (D) Kelli swam with the fairies.
    (E) all of the above

3. Which of the following answers was not in the story?
    (A) fairies
    (B) fairy godmother
    (C) happiness
    (D) rides
    (E) sweets

4. Kelli wished that her world was like the Land of
_____.
    (A) Butterflies
    (B) Fairies
    (C) Happiness
    (D) Rides
    (E) Sweets

Part 3: Stories 33–48 (2–3 pages each)

Story #45

Magic Carpet

Our class went on a special field trip. Our teacher, Miss Margaret, likes to reward us with surprises. Miss Margaret only told us that we were taking a field trip. We had no idea where we were going.

We expected a school bus to take us somewhere. When we arrived at school on the morning of the field trip, there was a very large, red carpet in the parking lot. We were surprised when Miss Margaret asked us all to sit on the carpet.

When we were all seated, a mysterious voice said, "Okay. It looks like you are all set to go."

Katie asked, "Who said that?"

"I did," answered the voice. "My name is Mike the Magic Carpet. I can talk and I can take you wherever you want to go. Where should I take you?"

All of the kids started talking at the same time.

"Let's go to the zoo," suggested Kristy.

Brian said, "To a museum."

"I want to go to the amusement park. That would be a good place for a magic carpet to go," mentioned Jeffrey.

Cathy offered, "The mall would be fun!"

"I say we go to the mountains so we can go snowboarding," said Mary Anne.

Sophie insisted, "No. Don't listen to them. Let's go to the beach. It would be a nice day to ride the waves."

"Let's watch a baseball game. The magic carpet can hover above the field. We'd have the best seats ever," said Reese.

Someone blew a whistle. We looked up and saw Miss Margaret. Her cheeks were red and she had a whistle in her mouth. It suddenly became very quiet. Our class had never seen Miss Margaret upset until now. We weren't even aware that our teacher had a whistle.

Miss Margaret calmly said, "Students, please stop arguing. It doesn't help when we all talk at the same time. I planned this field trip as a reward for good behavior. It sounds as though that may have been a mistake. I know you're excited about the magic carpet, but we need to calm down and quietly work together. Does anyone have a suggestion on how you can all agree on one place?"

Katie raised her hand. When Miss Margaret called on Katie, she suggested, "Let's narrow it down to three options and then vote on it."

Miss Margaret replied, "Okay. Let's try that."

We quietly worked together and came up with the top three choices. After we voted, Miss Margaret asked Katie to announce the winning choice.

Katie announced, "It looks like we're going to the mall."

Mike asked us to find our places on the carpet. "As soon as you are ready, we will leave."

The magic carpet slowly lifted up off the ground. As the carpet drifted over the school, our class waved to all the kids on the playground. The kids down below clapped and cheered when they saw us on the magic carpet.

Mike flew over the school and through our town. The word must have gotten out that there was a magic carpet flying over the town because many people came out to see us.

Miss Margaret had packed lunches for us. It was like having a picnic up in the sky. We ate lunch while drifting through the air.

When we arrived at the mall, Mike slowly descended the carpet in the large parking area. Miss Margaret asked us to form groups of four or more. She reminded us to behave well and have fun. We needed to return to the magic carpet by 2:30 p.m.

We had fun hanging out at the mall, but we were excited to get back on the magic carpet. We met Miss Margaret at 2:30 p.m. She walked us back to the magic carpet.

After we were all settled on the carpet, Mike asked, "What would you like to see before we fly back to school?"

This time after Mike asked a question, we took our time answering and we answered one at a time instead of all at once. We also stated our requests with our indoor voices.

Cathy said, "I would love to fly over my house."

"That's a good idea," commented Katie. "Wouldn't it be nice if we could fly over all of our houses?"

Mary Anne asked, "Why don't we take a vote to see what the others want?"

All of the students thought that was a good idea so we took a vote. We all voted to fly over our houses.

On our way back to school, Mike took us for a ride over each of our houses. It was fun looking at our homes from up above.

Miss Margaret told us how happy she was to see that we had learned to work together.

1. Mike is a _____.
    (A) bus driver
    (B) magic carpet
    (C) principal
    (D) student
    (E) teacher

2. The first place the students went to was _____.
    (A) a baseball game
    (B) an amusement park
    (C) the beach
    (D) the mall
    (E) the mountains

3. Which lesson did the students learn in this story?
    (A) It helps to work together.
    (B) It is important to be honest.
    (C) It is necessary to work hard.
    (D) The first answer wins.
    (E) The loudest answer wins.

4. Why did the class go on a field trip?
    (A) It was a reward for good behavior.
    (B) It was National Field Trip day.
    (C) One of their parents made a large donation.
    (D) The class won a contest.
    (E) The school was closed for remodeling.

Part 3: Stories 33–48 (2–3 pages each)

Story #46

The King's Ball

Kimmy Johansson,

You are cordially invited to attend the King's Ball. It will be held on Friday, March 3rd.

The Ladyship's golden carriage will pick you up at 3:00 p.m.

There will be prizes for the most creative and beautiful gowns. To participate, there are three rules. First, you must design your own gown. Second, you must select the fabric. Lastly, you must sew the gown yourself.

Sincerely.

King & Queen Hartford

This was a dream come true for Kimmy. She has wanted to be a fashion designer for as long as she can remember. She loves sketching her ideas on paper. She has often dreamed of designing a gown for the King's Ball.

Kimmy sat down at her desk and drew a sketch of her dream gown. It would have short sleeves, and it would be fitted through the bodice and waist. The skirt would be long and flowing.

Her favorite color is pink. Kimmy has been told that pink is the color best suited for her hair and complexion. She decided that the gown would be a light pink chiffon, with satin and lace. Hundreds of crystal beads would be sewn on the bottom eight inches of the shirt and around the neck.

Kimmy began making the pattern for her gown. She also figured out how much fabric she would need.

Her mother took her fabric shopping as soon as Kimmy was ready. Kimmy's mother knew that this project was very important to her daughter. Kimmy had fun selecting the fabric.

Kimmy worked on her gown every day. It took much time to cut and sew her gown. Kimmy was very excited when she was ready for her first fitting. She stood in front of her full-length mirror admiring her work. The gown fit almost perfectly. It just needed a few small alterations.

On the morning of March 3rd, Kimmy's mother took her to a beauty salon. Kimmy had her hair trimmed and styled. Then she got both a manicure and pedicure.

When they returned home, it was time for Kimmy to put her gown on. Her mother helped her with the finishing touches. Kimmy looked beautiful.

At 3:00 p.m. sharp, the Ladyship's golden carriage pulled up to Kimmy's house. The driver helped her into the carriage. Her mother took several pictures of Kimmy.

The carriage was drawn by two white horses. Kimmy could hardly wait to reach the King's Ball. It wouldn't be long now. She enjoyed the ride.

When the carriage arrived at the castle, Kimmy saw at least twelve other carriages. All of the girls were helped out of their carriages and led inside the castle. Each girl looked beautiful in her gown. Kimmy wondered how they would be able to pick just one winner. Every gown looked special. Kimmy decided that she would have fun no matter who the winner was.

One by one, the girls modeled their gowns while walking down a long spiral staircase. The judges asked each of the girls to tell them something about themselves. Kimmy told them how she had always wanted to be a fashion designer. She had often dreamed of being asked to attend the King's Ball, so this was truly a dream come true. Kimmy also told them that before the ball, all she could think about was winning. However, now that she was at the ball, she felt like she was a winner just for being there.

When it was time for the king to announce a winner, the room suddenly became very quiet. The king said, "I declare each and every one of you a winner. Each one of you went above and beyond what we expected from you. We have never seen so many talented girls compete in this contest. You should be very proud of your accomplishments. A trophy in the shape of a golden carriage will be awarded to each one of you. Congratulations! It is now time for you to enjoy a royal feast in your honor."

Dinner with the king and queen was exciting. The queen put the girls at ease by welcoming them to her dinner table. She told them to relax and enjoy the rest of the wonderful evening.

After dinner, the girls were led to the ball room. The band played a special song to congratulate them. The king danced the first dance with the queen, and then danced with each of the girls. The king moved effortlessly across the dance floor.

A cake in the shape of a princess wearing a gown was served. The girls enjoyed eating the sweet cake while chatting with the king and queen's daughter, Princess Penelope. The princess hugged the girls and told them how talented they all were.

1. What color was Kimmy's gown?
    (A) blue
    (B) green
    (C) pink
    (D) red
    (E) yellow

2. What color were the horses?
    (A) black
    (B) brown
    (C) gray
    (D) tan
    (E) white

3. Kimmy sewed _____ into her gown.
    (A) crystal beads
    (B) diamonds
    (C) gemstones
    (D) gold balls
    (E) silver rings

4. Who won the contest?
    (A) every girl
    (B) Karen
    (C) Katelyn
    (D) Kimmy
    (E) Princess Penelope

Part 3: Stories 33–48 (2–3 pages each)

Story #47

Glass-bottom Boat

My family took a glass-bottom boat tour. I thought it was better than watching television. We saw all kinds of ocean life through the glass.

First we saw fish swimming in an underwater garden. Some of the fish we saw were bright orange with white bands outlined in black. Our tour guide, Larry, called them clown fish. In a way, they sort of reminded me of a face painted on a circus clown.

When we saw sea lions, we actually got to feed them. We tossed anchovies and sardines to them over the railing. I secretly wanted to eat them, too, because I think anchovies taste great on pizza. I'm not sure about sardines though. I asked Larry if the sea lions would like pizza, but he said that they only eat meat. Larry told me not to share any pizza with them. That was easy because I didn't have any pizza.

It was scary when we saw a shark through the glass bottom. I was glad that we were on a boat, and not swimming in the water. The shark came right up to the glass window. He was looking at us while we were looking at him. It was scary to have a staring contest with a shark. My little brother, Luke, really enjoyed it. Luke still talks about it every day.

We saw an eel that lives in the rocks. If Larry hadn't pointed it out to us, we probably wouldn't have seen it. The eel blended in with the rocks. I thought that it looked like a snake. Larry said that it may look like a snake, but it really is a fish. Still, I wouldn't want to swim anywhere near it.

I was excited when I saw an octopus. Larry explained that an octopus isn't always easy to find. The pigment in the octopus' skin lets it match the colors of its surroundings.

The captain took us to a little island. We had a barbeque picnic on the island. We watched sea otters while we ate lunch. They looked cute when they swam on their backs. A few of them were lazing on the island. One looked silly when he wrapped himself in a kelp bed and fell asleep.

The best part of the tour was exploring the island after we ate our lunch. The girls went together to see what was on the other side of the island. It didn't take us long to get to the other side because the island was so small. We climbed the rocks along the shore. There was a nature-made water slide among the rocks. It was a fun way to cool off.

My sister, Stacy, called to us, "Come over here. I found a cave to explore."

We ran over to see what it was. The girls weren't sure if they should enter it. Stacy and I decided to be brave and check it out. We held hands as we slowly entered the cave.

Suddenly, someone said, "Hi, girls."

We almost jumped out of our shoes! We turned around to see who it was.

It was our older brother, Donald. Stacy and I each let out a breath of relief. That was even scarier than seeing the shark.

Part 3: Stories 33–48 (2–3 pages each)

After we calmed down, Donald showed us some really bright fish that were swimming in the water in the cave. I'm not sure what kind of fish they were, but I really enjoyed seeing those bright colors. Fortunately, the sun was shining from the right angle so that we could get a good look at them.

We returned to the glass-bottom boat just in time to get seated. My younger brother, Luke, was talking about how much fun he had watching sand crabs. He thought it was "so cool" watching them burrow themselves in the sand. I wanted to tell him about my day, but he wouldn't stop talking.

While Luke was busy talking, I saw a dolphin out the window. Stacy spotted the dolphin, too. Both of us stood up to get a better look. The dolphin made playful noises and did some tricks. It was quite exciting. Everybody else was so busy listening to Luke's story that they didn't see the dolphin before it swam away.

We saw many kinds of fish and another shark on the trip back. I never realized that a boat ride could be so much fun.

1. They got to feed _____.
    (A) an octopus
    (B) clown fish
    (C) eels
    (D) sea lions
    (E) sharks

2. Larry said that the eel is a kind of snake.
    (A) true
    (B) false

3. Who surprised the girls in the cave?
    (A) a mermaid
    (B) Donald
    (C) Larry
    (D) Luke
    (E) their parents

4. Most of the passengers didn't see the dolphin because _____.
    (A) Donald scared them.
    (B) It was very dark outside.
    (C) Larry was describing sea life.
    (D) Luke was telling a story.
    (E) The captain was making an announcement.

Part 3: Stories 33–48 (2–3 pages each)

Story #48

Reading Club

A club called Girls Love to Read meets every Tuesday evening. Members love to read, write, and discuss stories.

One Tuesday, Nicole started a discussion by asking, "Could reading too many fantastic stories be a bad thing?"

Alice asked a question about Nicole's question. "What do you mean? Everyone knows that reading is good. How could it be bad to read stories?"

Nicole explained what she meant. "We read about being princesses, meeting mermaids, going on grand adventures, and other incredible stories. Life seems so much better in those stories. One way that they might be bad is that it might make our real lives seem boring by comparison. Another way is that they might create expectations for ourselves that we can never live up to."

"Wow, Nicole," said Paige, "I never would have thought about it that way. That's interesting."

Everyone thought about this for a while. Then Suzie broke the silence. "For me, the great thing about fantastic stories is that they let me escape from reality. They take me somewhere wonderful. They help me get my mind off my problems. They relieve stress."

"Those stories give me hope," added Alison. "They give me reason to hope for a better world. They make me want to work to make the world a better place, even if I can only make a tiny difference."

Tiffany said, "Suzie and Alison made some great points. Sometimes, the characters suffer before they reach their happy endings. I enjoy the happy endings, but I really don't like reading bad parts."

"Neither do I," said Elizabeth, "but I suppose the pain and suffering is there to make the ending seem even happier."

"There might be another reason," offered Sarah. "Those parts of the story show us that everybody, even heroes, have problems and experience pain. Often, their problems are much worse than my problems. It helps me put things in perspective."

Crystal added, "That brings us back to Alison's idea of hope. When we read about characters overcoming difficult challenges, it offers us hope that we can face and solve our own problems."

Andrea asked, "Doesn't it sometimes seem like it's too far-fetched? I often read a story and think to myself that it could never happen like that in reality. Wouldn't it be helpful to read realistic stories? They might be easier to relate to. They might be more relevant for the problems we face."

"Wouldn't that be too boring?" asked Courtney. "Who would want to read a book about my life? My life is real, but it would never become a book."

"I would," said Tiffany. "You're on the basketball team. I would love to read about that."

"Thank you, Tiffany, but I don't think thousands of people would want to read about my life."

Part 3: Stories 33–48 (2–3 pages each)

Andrea said, "You never know what people will read. It could become a bestseller. Maybe you should start writing an autobiography."

Courtney laughed. Others offered encouragement and giggled, thinking how cool it would be for their friend to write a book.

After a moment, Alice said, "I still think reading is wonderful, whether it's fantastic or realistic. It helps with vocabulary, spelling, grammar, and even develops thinking skills."

"I think everyone is right," said Paige.

Elizabeth asked, "How can that be?"

Paige explained, "I think it's about achieving balance. Some fantasy shows you how good things can be and gives you hope. It provides an escape from your problems. Some realism helps you relate to the story better and it is more relevant to your own problems."

Nicole said, "That's a great idea, Paige. Everybody shared great ideas. Thank you all very much."

1. Nicole was concerned that reading fantastic stories might _____.
    (A) help improve spelling and grammar
    (B) make life seem boring
    (C) offer people hope
    (D) provide an escape from reality
    (E) show people how to overcome difficult challenges

2. Everyone agreed that reading fantastic stories is a bad idea.
    (A) true
    (B) false

3. Suzie suggested that fantastic stories help to _____.
    (A) demonstrate realism
    (B) develop thinking skills
    (C) offer hope
    (D) relieve stress
    (E) solve problems

4. Paige suggested that it may be good to _____.
    (A) find balance between fantasy and reality
    (B) look up words in the dictionary
    (C) only read fantastic stories
    (D) only read realistic stories
    (E) skip the bad parts of the book

THANK YOU!

We sincerely thank you for reading Julie Harper's book, *Reading Comprehension for Girls*.

Our team worked very hard on this book: Julie wrote the stories, an editor proofread them, a typographer formatted the interior, Melissa Stevens designed the cover and illustrated the book, and feedback from people like you helped develop the stories into their current shape.

Everyone on this team would be very appreciative if you would please share your feedback on this book in a review at Amazon, Goodreads, a blog (if you have one), or anywhere else you would feel comfortable expressing feedback.

We hope that your children or students enjoyed this book. Thank you very much for using it. ☺

ANSWER KEY

Answer Key

Story #1: Treasure Hunt
1. C
2. B
3. A
4. C

Story #2: Riding a Cloud
1. B
2. A
3. A
4. A

Story #3: Three Wishes
1. B
2. B
3. C
4. B

Story #4: Dream Fairies
1. A
2. A
3. B
4. A

Story #5: Basketball Girl
1. B
2. C
3. A
4. B

Story #6: Lucky Penny
1. A
2. B
3. C
4. B

Story #7: Mermaid Swim
1. A
2. C
3. B
4. B

Story #8: Fairyland
1. C
2. C
3. B
4. B

Story #9: Rescue Cat
1. C
2. A
3. B
4. B

Story #10: Star Gazer
1. C
2. A
3. B
4. A

Story #11: Princess of the Year
1. C
2. C
3. A
4. A

Story #12: Field Trip
1. C
2. C
3. B
4. B

Story #13: Fairy Night
1. B
2. A
3. C
4. B

Story #14: Dolphin Swim
1. A
2. A
3. A
4. C

Story #15: Pool Party
1. A
2. B
3. C
4. C

Story #16: Dream Flight
1. B
2. A
3. C
4. B

Story #17: Rainbow Fairy
1. A
2. D
3. B
4. B

Story #18: Slumber Party
1. B
2. F
3. A
4. E

Story #19: Golden Eagle
1. B
2. B
3. B
4. B

Story #20: Sweet Land
1. B
2. C
3. A
4. B

Answer Key

Story #21: Mermaid Friend
1. C
2. B
3. A
4. A

Story #22: Robot Design
1. C
2. B
3. D
4. A

Story #23: Birthday Surprise
1. C
2. B
3. B
4. A

Story #24: Harsh Words
1. C
2. D
3. D
4. A

Story #25: Best Friend
1. C
2. D
3. B
4. B

Story #26: Water Park
1. A, B, D
2. C, E
3. B
4. A

Story #27: Royal Feast
1. A
2. A
3. A
4. B

Story #28: Magic Bike
1. D
2. A
3. B
4. B

Story #29: Camping Scare
1. B
2. C
3. C
4. A

Story #30: Fashion Design
1. C
2. D
3. D
4. B

Story #31: Magic Time
1. C
2. B
3. C
4. A

Story #32: Special Glasses
1. B
2. E
3. B
4. A

Story #33: Mrs. Crabtree
1. C
2. E
3. D
4. B

Story #34: Island Magic
1. D
2. C
3. A
4. B

Story #35: Royal Ball—Part 1
1. B
2. A
3. A
4. A

Story #36: Royal Ball—Part 2
1. C
2. E
3. E
4. D

Story #37: Royal Ball—Part 3
1. A
2. B
3. B
4. D

Story #38: Slumber Mystery
1. D
2. A
3. A
4. D

Story #39: County Fair
1. E
2. B
3. A
4. A

Story #40: Mermaid Surprise—Part 1
1. C
2. A
3. D
4. B

Answer Key

Story #41: Mermaid Surprise—Part 2
1. E
2. C
3. C
4. B

Story #42: Mermaid Surprise—Part 3
1. A
2. B
3. A
4. C

Story #43: Martian Guide
1. A
2. D
3. B
4. B

Story #44: Fairy World
1. C
2. C
3. B
4. C

Story #45: Magic Carpet
1. B
2. D
3. A
4. A

Story #46: The King's Ball
1. C
2. E
3. A
4. A

Story #47: Glass-bottom Boat
1. D
2. B
3. B
4. D

Story #48: Reading Club
1. B
2. B
3. D
4. A

JULIE HARPER BOOKS

wackysentences.com

amazon.com/author/julieharper

Printing Practice:

    Printing Practice Handwriting Workbook for Girls.
    Printing Practice Handwriting Workbook for Boys.
    Tongue Twisters Printing Practice Writing Workbook.
    Print Uppercase and Lowercase Letters, Words, and Silly Phrases:
        Kindergarten and First Grade Writing Practice Workbook
        (Reproducible).
    Print Wacky Sentences: First and Second Grade Writing Practice
        Workbook (Reproducible).

Cursive Handwriting:

    Letters, Words, and Silly Phrases Handwriting Workbook (Reproducible):
        Practice Writing in Cursive (Second and Third Grade).
    Wacky Sentences Handwriting Workbook (Reproducible):
        Practice Writing in Cursive (Third and Fourth Grade).
    Cursive Handwriting Workbook for Girls.
    Cursive Handwriting Practice Workbook for Teens.
    Spooky Cursive Handwriting Practice Workbook.
    Cursive Handwriting Practice Workbook for Boys.

Reading & Writing:

    Reading Comprehension for Girls.
    Read Wacky Sentences Basic Reading Comprehension Workbook.
    Wacky Creative Writing Assignments Workbook.

Cursive Handwriting Workbook for Girls

Cursive Handwriting Practice Workbook for Teens

Made in the USA
Middletown, DE
03 January 2016